MANGO
magic

BayBooks

An imprint of HarperCollins*Publishers*

A Bay Books Publication

Bay Books, an imprint of
HarperCollins*Publishers*
25 Ryde Road, Pymble, Sydney, NSW 2073, Australia
31 View Road, Glenfield, Auckland 10, New Zealand

Published in Australia by Bay Books in 1987
This edition 1993

National Library of Australia
Card Number and ISBN 1 86256 114 1

Styling: Sarah Cottier
Food Preparation: Elizabeth Carden
Recipe development and testing: Glenda Holton
Design: Brett Cullen and Kim Falkenmire
Printed in Singapore

9 8 7 6 5 4 3 2 1
96 95 94 93

MANGO
MAGIC

Mouthwatering recipes for every occasion • Salads • Soups • Starters • Main Meals • Sweets • Drinks • Preserves

Photography Ashley Barber

BAY BOOKS
Sydney and London

Contents

Ham Steaks with Curried Mango Sauce • Eggs with Prawns and Mango • Ham Steaks with Maple Mango Sauce • Mango Pilaf • Spiced Chicken and Mango Curry • Mango Chicken Ginger • Chicken and Mango in Tarragon Wine Sauce • Chicken and Mango Risotto

SOMETHING TEMPTING 59

Fresh Fruit Tart • Mango Tart • Summertime Tart • Fresh Fruit Shortcake • Ginger Mango Cheesecake • Mango Cream Crepes • Mango Crepes with Sweet Wine Sauce • Mango Mille Feuille • Mango Eclairs • Mango Brown Betty • Mango Munch • Mango Souffle • Creamy Mango Mousse • Summer Fruit Meringue • Mango Chocolate Cups • Mango Lime Custard • Chilled Ginger and Mango Souffle • Mango Charlotte • Hot Ice Cream Balls and Mango Sauce • Mango Pecan Ice Cream • Mango, Passionfruit and Hazelnut Ice Cream • Cream Cheese and Mango • Mango Ice Cream • Tropical Island Sorbet • Mango Sorbet • Mango Lime Jelly with Passionfruit Sauce • Mango Parfait • After Dinner Mangos • Mango Delight • Fruit Compote • Tropical Fruit Salad with Mango Cream • Mango Sauterne • Fruits au Gratin

SUGAR AND SPICE 75

Macadamia and Mango Cake • Mango and Banana Cake • Favourite Fruit Cake • Mango Upside-down Cake • Tropical Fruit Cake • Mango-filled Roll • Mango and Date Slices • Mango Pecan Torte • Mango Coconut Log • Mango Layer Cake • Mango Bread • Mango Slices • Mango and Cinnamon Loaf • Mango Gingerbread

THE PANTRY SHELF 85

Mango Date Chutney • Hot Mango Chutney • Spicy Mango and Apple Chutney • Mango and Tomato Chutney • Mango Nectarine Chutney • Mango Nut Chutney • Mango Walnut Chutney • Mango Coulis • Mango Jam • Mango and Strawberry Jam • Mango Seafood Mayonnaise • Fresh Basil and Mango Vinaigrette • Spicy Mango Sauce • Mango Rhubarb Sauce • Mango Sauce • Honeyed Mango Sauce • Mango Garlic Sauce

SOMETHING COOL 90

Mango Mint Cooler • Tropical Mango Punch • Mango Coconut Ice • Mango Combo • Mango Rum Ice • Mango Treat • Tangy Mango Cooler • Minty Mango Whip • Champagne Mango • Mango Smoothie • Caribbean Mango • Ice Cream Mango Whip • Mango and Coconut Delight • Mango Milkshake • Mango Slimmer • Mango Punch Refresher • Mango Citrus Cup • Grand Marnier and Champagne Mango

FOR YOUR INFORMATION 94

INDEX 95

ACKNOWLEDGEMENTS 96

All about the Mango

The mango is one of the best-loved tropical fruits. Almost reflecting the warmth of the sun itself, the mango's golden flesh is deliciously succulent with a pleasing, firm texture and a sweet, yet tangy flavour. Simply sliced or diced, it's a treat to eat by itself or as an exotic addition to other foods.

Synonymous with summer, the mango often appears just in time to embellish salads and fruit salads or to serve as a cool, fruit drink.

Put into a blender, it's surprising how much juice can be extracted from one mango. And unlike many fruits, the mango keeps its thick consistency and distinctive flavour. Serve it 'au naturel' or add it to your favourite alcoholic base for a refreshing cocktail.

But there's no need to stop at salads and fruit drinks. The mango's perfection in the raw state often prevents cooks from recognising or experimenting with the fruit's potential in more elaborate dishes.

RECIPES FOR ALL TASTES

The variety of recipes in this book is an indication of the mango's great adaptability and versatility which we feel most cooks have not yet begun to exploit. With a mango or two on hand, you have the basis for any number of tempting meals, gourmet dishes, spectacular desserts and satisfying drinks as well as cakes, pastries and preserves.

We've presented recipes for all tastes and all occasions from exotic dishes you'll want to display at dinner parties to those informal, ready-in-a-jiffy meals for the whole family.

The succulent texture and golden warmth of the mango make it one of the best-loved tropical fruits

The mango is equally suitable in sweet or savoury creations as some of the world's gourmet chefs have discovered in recent years. It's no longer unusual to find the mango featured on the menus of top restaurants and hotels, served in piquant sauces to complement meat, poultry and game or as a puree or marinade with fish and other seafood dishes.

Because it has a highly individual flavour the mango makes a delicious, palate-pleasing accompaniment to both strong-tasting savouries like prosciutto or more bland alternatives like creamed cottage cheese.

As a dessert the mango by itself has few peers. It can be served in slices or cubed as a summer time favourite or combined with other fruits in a compote, flan, tart or torte. We've also added superb recipes for mango eclairs, parfait, souffle, mousse, sorbet and ice cream specialties.

Mango is not a fruit that readily comes to mind as the ingredient of a cake, pastry or crepe. Yet, its firm flesh is well suited to baking or even adding to a favourite fruit cake receipe. And mango is already well known as the basis for excellent jams, chutneys and preserves.

This easy to follow cookbook has been prepared to help you make the most of mangoes, in or out of season, to help you rediscover the fruit as the basis for a whole new range of dishes you'll be proud to display and keen to sample; food that will reflect your style and imagination. And we can promise you, these dishes are as easy and enjoyable to prepare as the finished product is to eat!

From bottom clockwise: Ginger Mango Cheesecake; Mango Crepes with Sweet Wine Sauce; Fresh Fruit Shortcake

THE MANGO STORY

With the botanical name of *Mangifera indica*, the mango belongs to the same family, *Anacardiaceae*, as the Jamaica plum and the cashew nut. It is a member of a genus made up of a dozen or so species of evergreen trees which are believed to be native to the East Indies and Malaya.

However, because it has been cultivated in India for more than 4000 years, the mango is also believed to be native to the Indian state of Assam. India produces the greatest amount of mangoes; five million tonnes are produced annually, most for home consumption and the fruit is connected with the folklore and religious ceremonies of that country.

Buddha himself was presented with a mango grove that he might find repose in its grateful shade. According to Hindu belief, the rich and succulent fruit sheltered the daughter of the sun as she was pursued by an evil sorceress.

Dr John Fryer, an employee of the East India Company who travelled to India and Persia in 1673, declared, after tasting the mango, that it was the world's most delicious fruit. 'For taste, the nectarine, peach and apricot fall far behind', he wrote.

The name mango is derived from the Tamil *man-kay* or *man-gay* which is the name the Portuguese adopted as *manga* when they settled in western India.

It is thought that Portuguese traders took the fruit on its worldwide travels to Africa and across to South America where it was probably introduced into Brazil.

Today, commercial growing is carried out in the West Indies, Central America, Africa, the Persian Gulf region, North and South America, Australia, the Philippines, Spain, Israel and in fact almost anywhere the climate permits.

CULTIVATING MANGOES

Mangoes grow on an evergreen tree which can be medium-sized or large, depending upon the conditions under which it is grown. Some grow tall and upright, others are round or oval-headed. Some trees have been known to reach a height of 27 metres with a spread of 38 metres.

The tree produces small pink flowers which grow in terminal panicles and are surprisingly light and dainty considering the size of the fruit ultimately produced. Blossoming takes place in early spring, but in some regions such as north Queensland, there are two flowering periods.

Although a tropical plant, the mango grows well in sub-tropical regions but will not tolerate areas where the rainfall is continuous. The tree prefers moderate moisture and appears to do best in regions where there is a definite dry season, ideally in spring. Heavy rains at the wrong time will cause the fruit to split.

Most soils are suitable for growing mangoes but the ground should be well cultivated, deep and well drained. Mangoes can be produced from seeds which should be freshly taken from the fruit and not allowed to dry out.

Often when a tree is grown from seed, it races away to form a long trunk which might become too tall for its allotted space. Fruit-laden branches also tend to droop to the ground. A gardener should keep these two points in mind.

It is also possible to buy grafted mango trees which bear fruit about three years after planting. These trees should be particularly well fed, particularly in their early years.

When mangoes are picked, a caustic sap squirts out from the fruit stalk. It can cause skin and eye irritations so gardeners are advised to wear sun glasses and rubber gloves when picking the fruit.

Mangoes are cultivated throughout the world and appear in many shapes and sizes

1   Slice pieces of mango lengthways off each side of the stone

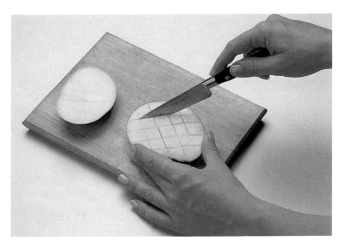

2   Score halves into cubes or diamonds

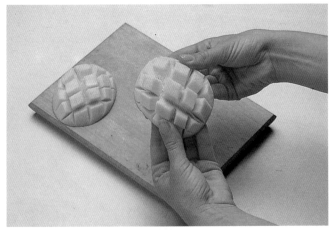

3   Flip inside out and eat

SOMETHING OF NUTRITIONAL VALUE

Mangoes can vary considerably in size, shape, colour, flavour and fibre content according to variety and maturity. Some are kidney-shaped while others are ovoid and beaked.

Usually large and heavy, mangoes can reach weights of 680 grams depending upon variety and quality. When raw they are green. When ripe, some are yellow-green, some are straw-coloured while others are orange or red.

The fruit is thin-skinned with fibrous sweet, well flavoured yellow to orange coloured flesh and a large clingstone. One of the best known Australian varieties is the apple mango or the Bowen or Kensington variety which weighs around 450 grams.

Its skin has a fine texture and is a bright orange with a rosy blush on the side which has been exposed to the sun. The flesh is deep orange and is free of fibres. When fully ripe this mango has a pleasant aromatic smell and is deliciously succulent. The aptly named Sensation is another new variety from Queensland's Atherton Tableland.

Mangoes are rich in vitamin A and contain significant quantities of vitamins B and C. The latter is reckoned to be at its greatest level when the mango is a little on the green side. While it is rather tart to eat raw at this stage, there is plenty to be said for selecting slightly under-ripe fruit with a firmer flesh and greater piquancy of flavour. Delay eating a mango for too long and it can take on a rather sickly flavour and woolly texture.

As a rule, the mango is ready to eat raw when the flesh under the tough skin feels slightly soft and pliant to the touch. It is possible to slow down the ripening process by wrapping mangoes in cling wrap and storing them in the cool crisper drawer of your fridge. Alternatively, hard and under-ripe fruit can be encouraged to soften and sweeten by keeping them in a warm spot.

HOW TO EAT A MANGO

On average, mangoes yield between 65 and 70 per cent of their weight in fruit. To some people, preparing and eating a mango seems more like an obstacle course than a pleasurable experience.

The culprit is the very large, oval clingstone which characterises the most popular varieties of this fruit. It sits in the centre of the mango and determinedly resists all attempts to separate it from the flesh as one might an avocado or peach.

The simplest solution is to locate the stone by inserting a thin, long-bladed knife and then slicing each 'cheek' lengthways off either side of the stone.

This technique does leave a fair amount of flesh attached to the stone but this can be scraped off for use in certain recipes or justifiably consumed on the spot as 'cook's perks'.

If the fruit is to be served raw, the two halves can be scored into cubes or diamonds, then simply flipped inside out and served immediately as an eye-catching dessert. The fruit should be eaten as soon after preparation as possible as it rapidly loses its attractive, distinctive aroma.

If you leave guests to tackle the fruit their own way, provide spoons and a small dessert knife. Finger bowls or moist towels and extra napkins should also be placed on the table.

COOKING WITH MANGOES

Mangoes which are not good enough to serve raw can be put into fools, chiffons, purees and sauces while chutneys, pickles and curries are useful destinations for under-ripe or slow-maturing fruit. Salted mango is popular in fish curries and here

again green fruit can be used. A jam recipe is the best solution for badly mangled mangoes.

For the great Aussie barbecue, a mango sauce to go with a barbecued steak or other beef dishes is delicious and easy to make.

Price may sometimes be off-putting for would-be mango cooks; sometimes out-of-season, imported fruit can be costly. However, with a little forward planning there is no reason why the mango should not be a feature of even humble, every-day meals throughout the year.

The trick is to make those delicious jams, chutneys and pickles when the fruit is cheap and plentiful and keep them stored. It also makes sense to prepare and freeze other suitable mango dishes and serve them when the fruit is scarce and costly. Such planning and inventiveness will be well rewarded by the surprise and delight of the family and dinner guests.

1   Peel skin from mango

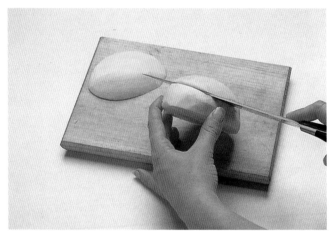

2   Cut thick slices from each side

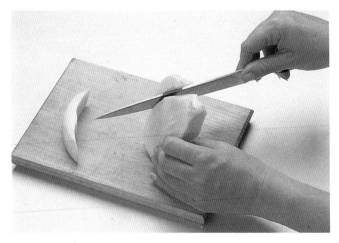

3   Remove remaining flesh

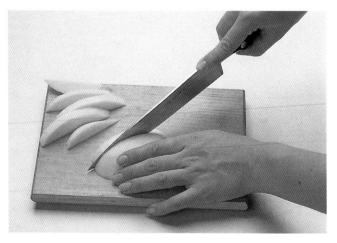

4   Slice into even-sized segments

Something Light

The mango's sweetness combined with its tangy taste adds flavour and piquancy to salads, soups and luscious light meals for hot days.

Just a few slices of mango or a tablespoon of mango puree will transform the simplest sauces and dressings into something extra special, light and definitely delicious.

Baked Mango with Crab

13

EXOTIC FLOWER SALAD

1 large or 2 small firm ripe
  mangoes
1 tablespoon lemon juice
1 tablespoon salad oil
salt, to taste
125 g button mushrooms,
  finely sliced
freshly ground pepper
1 large or 2 small
  mignonette lettuce
  leaves, washed and
  chilled
1 tablespoon chopped fresh
  herbs
2 tablespoons pine nuts,
  toasted
60 g snowpeas, topped,
  tailed and blanched
1 witloof, separated into
  leaves

French Dressing
2 tablespoons wine vinegar
1 teaspoon French mustard
salt and freshly ground
  pepper, to taste
6 tablespoons olive oil

Peel the mango and cut a thick slice from each side of stone and set aside for the salad.

Cut remaining flesh from stone and puree. Add lemon juice and oil and blench, adding salt to taste and adjusting the consistency for a creamy mayonnaise.

Combine mango mayonnaise, mushrooms, salt and pepper, and toss lightly.

Arrange lettuce leaves on plates in a flower shape with the mushrooms in middle. Sprinkle over the chopped herbs and nuts, arrange mango slices, snowpeas and witloof on the plate. Drizzle a little French Dressing on top and serve.

French Dressing: Mix the vinegar and mustard. Season to taste, then slowly whisk in the oil, beating constantly. Adjust seasoning if necessary.

Serves 6

CITRUS AND MANGO SALAD WITH CREAM DRESSING

1 lettuce
3 oranges, peeled and white
  pith removed
3 stalks celery, cut into
  8 cm pieces
450 g can mango slices,
  drained
1 cucumber, scored and
  sliced
6 shallots, finely sliced

Cream Dressing
¼ cup mayonnaise
⅓ cup cream
salt and freshly ground
  pepper, to taste
2 tablespoons chopped
  parsley
1 teaspoon French mustard
3 teaspoons orange juice
2 teaspoons lemon juice

Wash lettuce and arrange leaves on a large serving plate. Segment the oranges.

To make celery curls, slice the celery lengthways leaving one end uncut. Drop celery into iced water and leave until it curls.

Arrange mango slices, orange segments, celery curls and cucumber between lettuce leaves.

Garnish with shallots and refrigerate until ready to serve.

Cream Dressing: Mix all ingredients well, stand 15–20 minutes before using and serve separately.

Serves 6–8

TROPICAL FRUITS WITH LEMON RIND DRESSING

3 mangoes, peeled
2 avocados, peeled and
  seeded
4–6 lettuce leaves
2 bananas, peeled, sliced
  lengthways
90 g shelled macadamia
  nuts, chopped

Lemon Rind Dressing
1 teaspoon chopped lemon
  rind
1 tablespoon lemon juice
2 tablespoons olive oil
2 tablespoons safflower oil
cayenne pepper, to taste
salt, to taste

Cut a thick slice lengthways down each side of the mango stone, then slice lengthways into 4 pieces. Slice avocados into 5 or 6 slices.

Place lettuce leaves on serving plates and arrange the mango, banana and avocado slices decoratively on top. Drizzle with Lemon Rind Dressing and sprinkle over the macadamia nuts.

Lemon Rind Dressing: Blend dressing ingredients well and let stand 5–10 minutes.

Serves 4–6

Clockwise from front: Exotic Flower Salad; Tropical Fruits with Lemon Rind Dressing; Citrus and Mango Salad with Cream Dressing

MANGO RICE WITH CITRUS SALAD DRESSING

1½ cups cooked rice or ¾
    cup uncooked rice
1 medium-sized shallot,
    chopped
1 cup chopped celery
½ cup unsalted peanuts
1 medium-sized mango,
    peeled and chopped

Citrus Salad Dressing
½ cup fresh orange juice
juice 1 lemon
1 clove garlic, crushed
freshly ground pepper, to
    taste

Combine rice, shallot, celery, peanuts and mango. Pour dressing over salad, toss and serve.
Citrus Salad Dressing: Combine all dressing ingredients in a screw-top jar and shake well.
    Serves 4–6

MANGO TABOULI

1 cup burghul cracked
    wheat
2 cups diced mango
1 cup diced pineapple
5 shallots, finely chopped
½ cup finely chopped
    parsley
½ cup finely chopped mint
1 tablespoon lemon juice
salt and freshly ground
    pepper, to taste

Rinse burghul thoroughly then drain. Soak burghul in water to cover for 1 hour. Drain off any remaining liquid which has not been absorbed. Combine burghul with remaining ingredients, season to taste and stir through. Serve chilled.
    Serves 4–6

Left: Mango Rice with Citrus Salad Dressing;
right: Indian Mango Salad

INDIAN MANGO SALAD

1 large mango, peeled and
    diced
1 cup natural yoghurt
1 teaspoon wholegrain
    mustard
1 green chilli, very finely
    chopped or cayenne
    pepper, to taste
1 tablespoon desiccated
    coconut
salt, to taste
2 shallots, chopped

Prepare mango and set aside. Beat yoghurt in a bowl until smooth. Add mustard, chilli, coconut and salt. Stir in the mango and shallots. Serve chilled.
    Serves 4–6

BANANA AND MANGO TROPICANA

2 large mangoes, peeled,
    seeded and sliced
3 bananas, peeled
½ cup orange juice
pulp of 3 passionfruit
1 tablespoon brandy
1 tablespoon caster sugar

Place sliced mangoes and bananas in individual serving bowls.
    Combine orange juice, passionfruit pulp, brandy and caster sugar for the dressing in a screw-top jar and mix well until sugar is dissolved.
    Pour dressing over salad, toss lightly and serve.
    Serves 4

TURKEY, HAM AND MANGO SALAD

8 lettuce leaves, washed
8 slices cooked turkey
8 slices ham
2 mangoes, sliced
3 nectarines, halved and
    seeded
½ cup cottage cheese
1 capsicum, sliced
alfalfa sprouts, to garnish

Tear the leaves into bite-sized pieces and place on a large platter. Alternately layer turkey, ham and mango slices on lettuce leaves. Fill stone cavity of nectarines with a teaspoonful of cottage cheese. Place nectarines decoratively on platter, arrange capsicum slices on top and sprinkle over the alfalfa.
    Serves 6

REFRESHING SUMMER SALAD

4 chicken breast fillets
   (750 g), chopped
30 g butter
1 fennel bulb, washed and
   separated
¼ cup finely chopped
   shallots
2 mangoes, peeled and
   seeded
½ cup mayonnaise
salt and freshly ground
   pepper, to taste
finely chopped fresh
   fennel, to garnish

Heat butter and pan-fry chicken until tender and golden. Drain on absorbent paper and allow to cool. Chop fennel bulb into matchsticks and combine with chicken pieces and shallots in a salad bowl. Puree 1 mango with mayonnaise. Pour dressing over chicken mixture and season to taste.

Slice other mango. Garnish with mango slices and chopped fresh fennel.

Serves 6

Note: Substitute canned mango for fresh in this recipe if you prefer. One mango equals one can mango slices (450 g).

COCONUT MANGO SALAD

1½ cups chicken stock
3 chicken fillets (550 g)
3 carrots
¼ pineapple, peeled
2 mangoes, peeled
3 stalks celery
½ cup desiccated coconut,
   dry roasted

Garnish
basil leaves (optional)
pineapple top (optional)

Coconut dressing
½ tablespoon white wine
   vinegar
½ cup coconut cream
1 tablespoon oil
salt and freshly ground
   pepper, to taste

Bring chicken stock to boil, reduce heat and poach fillets 4–5 minutes until the flesh is opaque and tender. Allow to cool in the stock. When cool enough to handle, shred the chicken fillets. You may need to use your fingers to pull the fibres apart. While still warm, toss the chicken in dressing and set aside.

Leaving the stalks on if possible, peel the carrots with a fine potato peeler. Hold the stalk end firmly on a chopping board and peel the carrot to make long shreds, peeling only to the paler flesh. Arrange carrot shreds as a bed on individual serving plates.

Slice 6 thin slices of pineapple, then cut into pieces as fine as possible making petals. Fan the pineapple pieces in a circular fashion on top of the carrot shreds.

Cut the mango flesh into thin strips, arranging 4 or 5 pieces per plate, in star formation, in between the pineapple pieces.

Cut celery into fine julienne strips, and place in the centre of each salad.

Arrange the shredded chicken on top of celery to make a pyramid. Spoon over any remaining dressing and top with the roasted coconut. Garnish with basil leaves.

Coconut Dressing: Combine dressing ingredients in a screw-top jar and shake well.

Serves 4–6

CHICKEN AND MANGO WITH CURRY CREAM DRESSING

2 chicken breasts (375 g)
salt and white pepper, to
   taste
30 g butter
1 mango, peeled, seeded
   and sliced
2 stalks celery, cut in
   julienne
2 bananas, sliced and
   sprinkled with lemon
   juice
juice ½ lemon

Dressing
½ cup mayonnaise
¼ cup sour cream
1 tablespoon curry powder
30 g slivered almonds,
   toasted, to garnish

Skin the chicken breasts, season to taste and fry in butter on gentle heat, for 3 minutes each side until tender. Drain on absorbent paper. Cool, then slice diagonally into fine strips.

Combine chicken, mango, celery and banana in a bowl, then fold in the dressing. Allow to stand 15 minutes. Sprinkle with toasted almonds and serve.

Dressing: Combine mayonnaise with sour cream and curry powder.

Serves 4

Duck and Mango Combination

DUCK AND MANGO COMBINATION

This salad is best prepared as close to serving time as possible.

2–2.5 kg duck or 2 cups
   cooked duck meat
salt and freshly ground
   pepper, to taste
450 g green beans, chopped
2 red capsicums, cut in
   strips
1 mango, peeled and
   chopped
½ cup shelled macadamia
   nuts
1 × 225 g can lychees,
   halved
¼ cup lemon juice
½ cup oil
chopped parsley, to garnish

Wipe duck with a damp cloth and season inside and out with salt and pepper. Prick the skin with a fork to drain off fat during cooking. Truss and place on a rack in a roasting pan. Roast in an oven preheated to 180°C (350°F) for 2 hours until tender. Drain fat from pan as necessary.

Remove duck from oven, discard string and return to oven for 10 minutes. Take out and allow to cool, then remove meat, discarding skin, fat and bones. Cut into bite-sized pieces and set aside.

Blanch beans in boiling water, then simmer, uncovered for 4 minutes after water boils again. Drain, then rinse under cold, running water and drain again.

Blanch capsicums in boiling water a few minutes, drain, refresh under cold running water and drain again.

Combine all ingredients in a bowl, tossing until well mixed. Serve at room temperature.

Serves 8–10

SKEWERED MANGO SALAD

In Thailand this would be made with green mangoes. If these are not readily available, substitute with tart green apples.

300 g pork fillet, thinly
    sliced
1 tablespoon peanut oil
4 cloves garlic, crushed
6 shallots, sliced
1 tablespoon dried prawn
    powder
1 tablespoon Thai fish
    sauce
2 tablespoons roasted
    peanuts, crushed
1 teaspoon sugar
pepper, to taste
3 red chillies, seeded and
    finely sliced
3 cucumbers, seeded and
    grated
1 mango, peeled and finely
    sliced
1 cos lettuce, washed and
    divided into leaves
1 butter lettuce

Soak 12 bamboo skewers in boiling water for 10 minutes, then remove. Thread pork fillet onto skewers. Combine oil, garlic, shallots, prawn powder, fish sauce, peanuts, sugar, pepper and chillies and brush over the skewered pork.

Place under a moderate grill and cook 10 minutes. Combine remaining salad ingredients and arrange on serving plates. Arrange the pork skewers over the salad and serve.
    Serves 4

PORK SALAD WITH GINGER MANGO DRESSING

1 lettuce, washed and
    drained
½ pineapple, peeled and
    chopped
4 stalks celery, sliced
600 g pork fillet, fried and
    sliced into medallions
100 g hazelnuts, toasted
100 g mushrooms
1 mango, peeled, seeded
    and chopped or 450 g
    can mango slices
1 red apple, sliced and
    sprinkled with lemon
    juice to prevent
    browning

Above: Skewered Mango Salad; below: Pork Salad with Ginger Mango Dressing

snipped chives, to garnish
salt and freshly ground
    pepper, to taste
Ginger Mango
    Dressing
2 mangoes, peeled and
    seeded
⅔ cup mayonnaise
1 teaspoon ginger

Separate lettuce leaves, reserving a few large leaves to line salad bowl. Mix together remaining ingredients, season to taste, then spoon into serving bowl. Add dressing, garnish with chives and serve.
Ginger Mango Dressing: Puree mango, mayonnaise and ginger until smooth.
    Serves 4–6

PORK AND MANGO SALAD

Cold cooked turkey could also be added to this salad.

1 large mango, peeled
250 g cold cooked pork
2 cups chopped celery
1 shallot, finely chopped
½ cup almonds, toasted
salt and freshly ground
    pepper, to taste
6 lettuce leaves

Cut flesh from the mango into small cubes. Cut pork into bite-sized pieces. Combine mango, pork, celery, chopped shallot and almonds. Season to taste and toss well. Line salad bowl with lettuce leaves. Spoon mango and pork mixture onto lettuce. Chill before serving.
    Serves 4

TANGY MANGO AND HAM SALAD

1 mango, peeled and sliced
3 shallots, finely chopped
1 green capsicum, chopped
6 fresh or dried dates
2–3 tablespoons French
    dressing
1 mignonette lettuce
8 slices ham

Cut the mango slices into cubes, then combine with shallots and capsicum. If using fresh dates, remove the skin, cut in half, discard the seed and halve again. If using dried dates, chop finely. Add dates to the mango mixture. Toss with French dressing then chill.

To serve, arrange the lettuce leaves on a flat platter and place ham slices, either rolled or flat, around the edges. Spoon mango salad into the centre.
    Serves 4

MANGO COCKTAIL SALAD WITH CREAMY PARSLEY DRESSING

3 rashers bacon, chopped
2 mangoes, peeled and
  sliced
½ cup walnut halves
½ lettuce, shredded
salt and freshly ground
  pepper, to taste
2 avocados, peeled, seeded
  and halved

Creamy Parsley
  Dressing
¼ cup olive oil
2 tablespoons lemon juice
2 teaspoons finely chopped
  parsley
1 teaspoon French mustard
1 tablespoon thickened
  cream
1 clove garlic, crushed

Fry bacon until crisp, then drain on absorbent paper. Combine mangoes, walnut halves, bacon and lettuce.

Pour dressing over the salad, season to taste then toss.

Spoon the salad into the avocado halves. Arrange on serving plates and serve.

Creamy Parsley Dressing: Combine all ingredients for the dressing in a screw-top jar and shake well.

Serves 6

MANGO SEAFOOD SALAD

¼ small watermelon,
  seeded
1 small mango
2 grapefruit, peeled and
  segmented
2 kiwi fruit, peeled and
  sliced
210 g can mandarin
  segments, drained
250 g cooked and peeled
  prawns
salt and freshly ground
  pepper, to taste
lettuce leaves
¾ cup French dressing
lemon slices, to garnish

Form watermelon into balls with a melon baller or dice. Combine with remaining fruits and prawns. Season lightly, cover and chill.

To serve, spoon salad into a serving bowl lined with lettuce leaves. Pour over dressing, garnish with lemon slices and serve.

Serves 4–6

Mango Cocktail Salad with Creamy
Parsley Dressing

AVOCADO FILLED WITH MANGO CRAB

100 g can crabmeat,
*   drained*
1 small mango, peeled and
*   sliced*
100 mL sour cream
1 shallot, finely chopped
1 teaspoon lemon juice
2 teaspoons brandy
good pinch paprika
salt and freshly ground
*   pepper, to taste*
8 lettuce leaves, washed
*   and dried*
2 avocados, peeled and
*   seeded*
dill sprigs and cherry
*   tomatoes, to garnish*

Mash the crabmeat and mango together. Add the sour cream, shallot, lemon juice, brandy, paprika, salt and pepper, and blend well together.

Make a bed of lettuce leaves on a flat serving dish. Place an avocado half on the leaves and fill with the crab mixture. Chill for at least 1 hour before serving. Garnish with dill sprigs and cherry tomatoes.
    Serves 4

SEASIDE SALAD

1 small bunch spinach,
*   washed well*
450 g cooked prawns,
*   shelled and deveined*
½ cup French dressing
3 oranges, peeled and
*   segmented*
450 g roast pork, sliced into
*   strips*
dill sprigs, for garnish
1 pineapple, peeled and
*   sliced into 12 pieces*
1 mango, diced
salt and freshly ground
*   pepper, to taste*
mayonnaise, to serve

Line a serving bowl with spinach leaves. In a bowl, marinate prawns in French dressing for 30 minutes, then drain. Arrange prawns in an outer half circle on spinach leaves. Arrange orange segments to complete circle. Place pork strips in centre and garnish with dill sprigs.

Place pineapple slices and mango cubes decoratively, season lightly and serve with mayonnaise.
    Serves 4

PRAWNS, CORIANDER AND MANGO APPETISER

1 large mango, peeled
1 kg cooked king prawns,
*   peeled, leaving tails on*
salt and freshly ground
*   pepper, to taste*
juice 2 limes or 1 lemon
fresh coriander, to garnish

Slice mango evenly into 8 slices. Arrange mango around the outside of a plate with prawns in the centre. Season with salt and pepper, sprinkle with lime juice and decorate with coriander leaves.
    Serves 4

SPRINGTIME SALAD WITH TOMATO GHERKIN DRESSING

1 large lettuce, washed and
*   finely shredded*
450 g cooked crabmeat
2 mangoes, peeled
4 eggs, hard-boiled and
*   peeled*
2 tablespoons snipped
*   chives or finely chopped*
*   whole shallots, with*
*   green stalks*
salt and freshly ground
*   pepper, to taste*

Tomato Gherkin
    Dressing
½ cup mayonnaise
¼ cup French dressing
2 teaspoons finely chopped
*   gherkin*
1 tablespoon tomato sauce
1 teaspoon lemon juice

Pile lettuce on 4 plates and place crabmeat in the centre.
    Cut the mango flesh from either side of stone then slice thinly. Arrange the flesh around the crab.
    Separate the whites and yolks of the eggs. Press yolks through a sieve and sprinkle over crab. Finely chop the whites and sprinkle around the lettuce. Season to taste and garnish with chives. Serve the dressing with the salad.
Tomato Gherkin Dressing: Combine all ingredients for the dressing in a screw-top jar and shake.
    Serves 4

Above. Mango Seafood Salad; below: Avocado filled with Mango Crab

BAKED MANGO WITH CRAB

150 g crabmeat or 1 small
  cooked mud crab
½ teaspoon Cointreau or
  any orange-flavoured
  liqueur
1 teaspoon Grand Marnier
1 tablespoon sour cream
1 teaspoon grated lemon
  rind
salt and freshly ground
  pepper, to taste
1 medium-sized mango

Combine the crab, Cointreau, Grand Marnier, sour cream, lemon rind and seasoning together. Mix well.

Wash mango and cut lengthwise to the seed. Gently twist each half back and forth to loosen the flesh from the seed. It may be necessary to insert a small, sharp knife in between the flesh and the seed to separate the halves.

Spoon the crab mixture into each mango half, spreading the mixture on the surface also. Place on a baking tray and bake in a pre-heated oven at 180°C (350°F) for approximately 15 minutes.

Delicious as an entree served with cucumber and orange slices and crusty fresh bread.

Serves 2

SEAFOOD MANGO MOULD

12 medium-sized, cooked
  Balmain bugs
3 kiwi fruit, sliced
½ cup shallots, chopped
  and sauteed
1 mango, chopped
¼ cup ricotta cheese
1½ cups cooked rice
2 teaspoons Cointreau
salt and freshly ground   *1 tablespoon gelatine*
  pepper, to taste   *½ cup hot fish stock*

Remove meat in one piece from shells of Balmain bugs by splitting the tails. Arrange 4 pieces in a star pattern on the base of a greased mould and place layers of 2 sliced kiwi fruit between. Chop up remaining bugs and combine in a bowl with shallots, mango, ricotta cheese, rice, Cointreau, salt and pepper.

Dissolve gelatine in the fish stock and add half to the seafood mixture, mixing well to combine. Pour 2 tablespoons liquid into the mould, spoon seafood mixture on top, pressing down firmly and pour over remaining liquid. Fit a plate inside mould on top of seafood mixture, place a heavy object on top of the plate and refrigerate for at least 6 hours.

To unmould, run a knife around the edge to loosen, then invert on a serving platter. Garnish with kiwi fruit and serve.

Serves 6

POACHED SCALLOPS WITH MANGO, MELON AND SNOW PEAS IN SESAME DILL DRESSING

12 uncooked fresh scallops
25 g pickled ginger,
  chopped
2 tablespoons dry white
  wine
salt and freshly ground
  pepper, to taste
100 g snow peas, blanched
  and chopped
1 small honeydew or rock
  melon, scooped into balls
  with a melon baller
1 mango, peeled and thinly   **Sesame Dill Dressing**
  sliced   *juice 1 lemon*
6 cherry tomatoes, halved   *2 teaspoons chopped dill*
4 asparagus spears, halved   *3–4 drops sesame oil*
  lengthways and cooked   *vegetable oil*

Marinate the scallops with ginger for 20 minutes. Blanch scallops and ginger in white wine for 1 minute then cool. Drain to remove all pickling solution and season to taste.

Toss all ingredients except asparagus in Sesame Dill Dressing. Arrange the salad evenly on 4 chilled plates and garnish with asparagus spears.

Sesame Dill Dressing: Combine lemon juice, dill and sesame oil in a measuring cup. Top with oil to bring up to 150 mL. Pour into a screw-top jar and shake well till combined.

Serves 4

NEPTUNE'S SALAD

Makes a delicious entree for 4 or a light meal for 2 people.

2 small lobster tails, cooked
  and sliced into
  medallions
12 king prawns, cooked
  and peeled
170 g can crabmeat,
  drained
1 mango, sliced then diced
  without cutting through
  skin
1 carrot, julienned
1 cucumber, julienned
juice 1 lemon
salt and freshly ground
  pepper, to taste

Carefully combine all ingredients. Pour over the lemon juice and season. Chill well and serve.

Serves 4

Above: Poached Scallops with Mango, Melon and Snow Peas in Sesame Dill Dressing; below: Neptune's Salad

TANGY MANGO AND CUCUMBER SOUP

3 shallots, ends removed
1 mango, peeled, seeded
  and pureed
½ cup lemon juice
½ cup orange and mango
  juice
½ cup natural low-fat
  yoghurt
1 clove garlic, crushed
1½ cucumbers, peeled,
  seeded and grated
salt and freshly ground
  pepper, to taste
½ red capsicum, finely
  diced

In a blender process shallots, mango, lemon juice, orange and mango juice, yoghurt and garlic. Transfer to a serving bowl, add grated cucumber and season.

Chill until ready to serve. Garnish with sliced cucumber and finely diced capsicum.

Serves 4

MILD CURRY AND MANGO SOUP

1 mango, peeled and flesh
  removed or 450 g can
  mango slices
2 cups chicken stock
juice ½ lemon
¼ teaspoon curry powder
salt and freshly ground
  pepper, to taste
1 teaspoon saffron threads,
  to garnish

Puree mango with stock and lemon juice until smooth. Add curry powder and gently heat soup until hot. Do not allow to boil. Season and add cream before serving.

If serving cold there is no need to cook the soup, just puree with the seasoning and cream.

Serve with croutons or crusty bread and garnish with a few saffron threads.

Serves 4

Above: Tangy Mango and Cucumber
Soup; below: Mild Curry and Mango
Soup

Something Special

When you're searching for that dish with a difference, something that smacks of invention and imagination, then add dash with a mango.

This exotic and individual fruit is increasingly finding its way onto the menu as an arresting accompaniment to shellfish, a tangy contrast to cheese and a strikingly novel balance to beef, lamb, poultry and game.

With the imaginative presentation they deserve, these special savoury mango dishes will form the centrepiece for a meal to remember.

Partridge with Creamy Mango Coulis

DEVILLED MANGO CRAB

2 tablespoons fresh white
   breadcrumbs
1 tablespoon grated
   Parmesan cheese
2 tablespoons chopped
   parsley
40 g butter
6 shallots, chopped
250 g crabmeat, canned or
   fresh (cartilage removed)
2 tablespoons dry sherry
1 cup fresh white
   breadcrumbs
few drops Tabasco sauce
5 tablespoons pawpaw and
   mango chutney
salt and freshly ground
   pepper, to taste
knobs of butter, for baking
lemon slices and watercress
   sprigs, to garnish

To prepare the topping, combine breadcrumbs, cheese and parsley and set aside.

Heat butter in a small pan, then add shallots and fry until soft. Add crabmeat, sherry, breadcrumbs, Tabasco sauce, pawpaw and mango chutney. Season to taste. Stir well to combine. Cook over a low heat until heated through.

Divide mixture between 4 individual serving dishes or scallop shells. Sprinkle over the topping. Put 2 or 3 knobs of butter on top of each dish and bake in an oven preheated to 200°C (400°F) for 10 minutes. Serve garnished with lemon slices and watercress sprigs.

Serves 4

CRAYFISH PLATTER WITH MANGO AND AVOCADO

2 crayfish tails, cooked and
   cut into medallions
4 mangoes, peeled, seeded
   and sliced
2 avocados, peeled, seeded
   and sliced
½ very ripe mango or ½ ×
   420 g can mango slices,
   drained
2 tablespoons sunflower oil
1 tablespoon lemon juice
salt and freshly ground
   pepper, to taste
dry mustard, to taste

On a large platter, arrange crayfish, interspersed with mango and avocado. Combine the very ripe mango, oil and lemon juice. Season with pepper and mustard.

Puree and pour over lobster and fruit.

Serves 6

CRAYFISH WITH MANGO AND FRESH BASIL VINAIGRETTE

2 uncooked crayfish tails
2 mangoes, peeled and
   thinly sliced

Court Bouillon
1 cup water
1 cup white wine
2 bay leaves
3 stalks parsley
4 peppercorns
1 onion, sliced
1 small carrot, sliced
1 stalk celery, chopped
salt, to taste

Fresh Basil Vinaigrette
bunch fresh basil
1 clove garlic
2 tablespoons wine vinegar
6 tablespoons oil
salt and freshly ground
   pepper, to taste

Place all ingredients for court bouillon in a saucepan. Bring to the boil, then simmer, covered, for 20 minutes; strain.

Bring court bouillon to boil. Add crayfish tails and simmer for 5–10 minutes until shells turn red. Remove tails and when cool, peel off shells and cut flesh into 1 cm thick medallions.

Fresh Basil Vinaigrette: Puree basil leaves, garlic, vinegar and oil and season to taste.

To assemble, first arrange a circle of mango slices on 4 plates. In the centre, place lobster and pour over the sauce.

Serves 4

Left: Devilled Mango Crab; right:
Crayfish Platter with Mango and Avocado

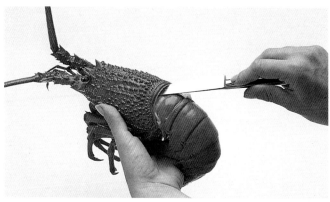

1   Slip knife under head to loosen it from body

2   Twisting gently pull head from body

3   Cut towards tail on underside of shell

4   Loosen meat; slice into medallions

Mango and Prawn Salad

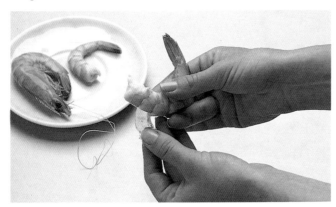

1 Remove head, shell and legs of prawn

2 Make a small cut to expose vein above tail

3 Pull vein through

4 Place in bowl of water until wanted

MANGO AND PRAWN SALAD

12 prawns, shelled and
  deveined
2 mangoes, peeled
125 g snow peas
4 shallots, chopped
1 cup pecans
2 tablespoons French
  dressing
salt and freshly ground
  pepper, to taste

Clean prawns and halve if large. Cut a large slice from each side of the mango stone, then cut away the remaining flesh. Cut the large mango slices into strips.

Blanch snow peas into boiling water for 1 minute. Drain and cool under cold running water. If preferred snow peas can be served raw in the salad.

Combine prawns, mango, snow peas, shallots and pecans. Pour over French dressing, season to taste, toss well and serve.

Serves 4–6

FISH IN MANGO SAUCE

1½ teaspoons ghee or
  clarified butter
1 large onion, finely sliced
1 tablespoon cornflour
1 cup water
⅔ cup mango pulp (1–2
  mangoes pureed)
1 kg jewfish, cut in 2½ cm
  slices
salt, to taste
1–2 tablespoons chopped
  coriander leaves, to
  garnish

Masala Paste
1 tablespoon coriander
  seeds
6 cloves garlic
2 red chillies, seeded
2.5 cm piece ginger root
2.5 cm piece coconut flesh

Combine all masala paste ingredients together in blender or food processor.

Heat ghee and fry paste for 1 minute. Add onion and saute for 3–4 minutes stirring. Blend cornflour to a paste with a little water, then add remaining water. Combine with onion and stir well. Pour in mango pulp and bring to boil, stirring frequently then add fish. Season to taste with salt. Simmer on low heat 15–20 minutes until fish is cooked. Garnish with coriander leaves and serve hot.

Serves 4

TROPICAL SEAFOOD SALAD WITH DILL VINAIGRETTE

2 small lobsters, cooked
500 g scallops, trimmed
2 teaspoons oil
2 bananas, peeled and
  thinly sliced diagonally
6 small zucchini, julienned
1 soft-skinned cucumber,
  unpeeled and julienned
6 medium-sized carrots,
  julienned
salt and pepper,
  to taste
1 mango, peeled and sliced
1 ripe honeydew melon,
  finely sliced
chopped basil, to garnish
1 cup cherry tomatoes, to
  garnish

Dill Vinaigrette
2 tablespoons white wine
  vinegar
1 tablespoon chopped dill
2 tablespoons vegetable oil
salt and freshly ground
  pepper, to taste

Remove lobster tails from shells and slice finely; toss in 1 tablespoon Dill Vinaigrette and set aside. Remove the legs from the shell. Slice scallops into 3 thin rounds. Heat oil in a pan and fry scallops for 1 minute. Drain scallops, sprinkle with a little vinaigrette and set aside.

Toss bananas, zucchini, cucumber and carrots together in a little vinaigrette. Season to taste.

Arrange slices of mango and honeydew melon around each plate with pieces of banana in between. Arrange the zucchini mixture in the centre of the plate and spoon the scallop and lobster meat on top.

Arrange basil leaves and cherry tomatoes around the edge. Arrange a lobster claw on one side and serve.

Dill Vinaigrette: Mix all the vinaigrette ingredients thoroughly together in a screw-top jar and season to taste.

Serves 6

VEAL SCALLOPINI WITH MANGO CREAM SAUCE

130 g butter
1 mango, peeled, seeded
    and diced
4–6 slices stale white bread,
    crusts removed
4–6 slices veal fillets (each
    100–140 g)
nutmeg, to taste
½ cup white wine
⅓ cup cream
salt and freshly ground
    pepper, to taste

Melt 40 g butter in a heavy-based pan, add mango and cook, covered, over gentle heat for 5–8 minutes. Set aside.

Heat 50 g butter in another pan and fry the bread on both sides. Remove and keep warm. In the same pan heat remaining butter. When it starts to foam, reduce heat and fry veal pieces on both sides for 2–3 minutes. Pour off excess butter, add the wine and bring it to the boil. Continue cooking 1 minute, turning veal once.

Add cream and mango to the pan and allow to thicken over low heat. Season with salt and pepper to taste. Arrange each slice of veal on a slice of fried bread and carefully pour over the sauce.

Serves 4

MANGO HAZELNUT VEAL

100 g mango flesh, roughly
    chopped
100 g fresh white
    breadcrumbs
50 g hazelnuts, finely
    chopped
1 tablespoon finely
    chopped parsley
50 g butter
1 small onion, finely
    chopped
finely grated rind and juice
    1 orange
1 egg, beaten
salt and freshly ground
    pepper, to taste
1.5 kg veal breast, boned

Combine mango, breadcrumbs, hazelnuts and parsley, and mix well.

Melt the butter in a saucepan and fry the onion gently until tender. Remove from heat and stir in the mango and breadcrumb mixture. Add orange rind and juice, beaten egg and season to taste. Mix thoroughly.

Form an opening in the veal by inserting a knife blade between the 2 layers of muscle. Lay the breast skin-side down and fill opening with the stuffing. Secure the top flap of flesh firmly under stuffing to form a neat roll.

Draw the 2 long edges of the breast together over the opening and sew up the edges with needle and white cotton.

Place veal into an oven preheated to 180°C (350°F) and slow roast for 1¼ – 1½ hours, basting every 20 minutes. Remove stitches and serve either hot or cold.

Serves 6–9

SKEWERED MANGO BEEF

¾ cup mango and pawpaw
    chutney
6 slices topside steak, finely
    pounded
2 cups wholemeal
    breadcrumbs
1 teaspoon oregano
salt and freshly ground
    pepper, to taste
75 g butter
1 onion, finely chopped
1 shallot, finely sliced
1 tablespoon oil
2 tablespoons cornflour
2 tablespoons tomato paste
440 g can beef consomme
1 mango, sliced
750 g can pineapple, sliced,
    drained or
½ pineapple, peeled and
    sliced

Spread ½ cup mango and pawpaw chutney evenly over the top of each steak.

Combine breadcrumbs with oregano and season to taste. Heat butter in a frying pan, add onion and shallot and cook for 2 minutes. Mix into the breadcrumb mixture and spread over the steaks and chutney. Roll up and secure with toothpicks.

Wipe the pan clean, add oil and brown the beef on all sides. Cover and cook over medium heat for 6 minutes.

Blend cornflour and tomato paste. Add remaining chutney and gradually stir in the beef consomme. Bring to boil in a small saucepan, stirring constantly. Pour over the beef, cover and simmer a further 6–8 minutes. Remove toothpicks and serve with fresh mango or pineapple.

Serves 6

ROSEMARY LAMB IN PUFF PASTRY

1 fresh mango, peeled and
   sliced or 450 g can
   mango, drained
1 tablespoon rosemary
1 tablespoon chopped
   parsley
2 cloves garlic, finely
   chopped
1–2 tablespoons apricot jam
   or mango jam (see recipe)
1 small onion, finely
   chopped
1 loin lamb, boned and
   trimmed of excess fat
60 g butter
500 g packet frozen puff
   pastry, thawed
1 egg, lightly beaten
1 tablespoon milk

Cut mango into thin slices and set aside. Blend well with
the herbs, garlic, jam and onion. Spread most of this mixture over the lamb. Roll up, securing with skewers and tie
the lamb every 2.5 cm with string.

Heat butter in a heavy-based pan and brown lamb on all
sides. Cool, remove strings and set aside.

Roll out pastry so it is large enough to completely
enclose lamb, with an additional 2 cm overlap. Spread
remaining stuffing thinly over inside of pastry. Wrap lamb
and decorate pastry with cut-out pastry leaves; brush over
with combined egg and milk. Roast in an oven preheated
to 260°C (500°F) for 25 minutes for medium rare lamb, 35
minutes for medium lamb. Let stand 15 minutes before
carving.

Serves 4–6

MANGO CHICKEN DELIGHT

30 g butter
1 onion, finely chopped
1 clove garlic, crushed
200 g ham, minced
200 g bacon, minced
1 egg, lightly beaten
1 teaspoon mixed herbs
salt and freshly ground
    pepper, to taste
4–6 fresh spinach leaves
1.8 kg boned chicken, left
    whole
½ mango, peeled, seeded
    and sliced
2 tablespoons oil

Melt butter in pan and fry onion and garlic until tender. Combine ham, bacon, onion mixture, egg, herbs, salt and pepper and mix thoroughly.

Spread 2–3 spinach leaves over chicken. Place half the ham-bacon mixture down centre, arrange mango slices in a single row on top, cover with remaining ham-bacon mixture, then with remaining spinach leaves. Roll up the chicken and sew flesh using a trussing needle and dark thread. Tie with string at 5 cm intervals to keep shape while cooking.

Place in a baking dish with oil and bake uncovered, in an oven preheated to 180°C (350°F) for 1½ hours, basting often with pan juices. Remove chicken, stand 10 minutes before slicing. Can be served hot or cold.

Serves 6–8

MANGO CHICKEN FETTUCINE

30 g butter
8 onions, peeled and
    chopped
1½ tablespoons flour
2 cups chicken stock
425 g can mango slices
450 g cooked chicken,
    cooled and chopped
salt and freshly ground
    pepper, to taste
850 g red fettucine noodles
850 g green fettucine
    noodles
1 tablespoon olive oil
125 g chopped walnuts
chopped basil, to garnish

Melt butter in pan and saute onions until golden. Add flour and cook for 1 minute. Gradually add chicken stock and bring to boil. Stir until the sauce thickens slightly. Simmer, covered, for 20 minutes. Add mango and chicken to saucepan and season to taste. Heat through.

Put pasta and oil into a large pan of salted, boiling water. Boil for 5–7 minutes or until cooked al dente. Drain in a colander, rinse in hot water and drain again. Combine pasta and walnuts with sauce and mix well. Serve on heated plates, garnished with basil.

Serves 6

SPICY CHICKEN AND MANGO

2 chicken breasts, halved
80 g ghee or clarified butter
1 small onion, finely
    chopped
4 cardamom pods
1 teaspoon nutmeg
½ cup water
8 slices of canned mango

Marinade
¾ cup yoghurt
1 tablespoon coriander
1 teaspoon ginger root,
    finely chopped
1 teaspoon salt
1 teaspoon turmeric
¼ teaspoon freshly ground
    black pepper

Remove all small rib bones from the chicken, leaving the large breastbone. Combine marinade ingredients in a bowl, add chicken, coat well and marinate in refrigerator a minimum of 2 hours or overnight.

Heat 60 g ghee in a pan. Fry onion, cardamom and nutmeg for 5 minutes until onion is tender. Add water, stir well and remove from heat.

Drain chicken breasts and reserve marinade. Place chicken in a baking tray and spoon onion mixture on top of each breast, then top with 2 slices mango. Dot with remaining ghee and bake in an oven preheated to 200°C (400°F) for 10 minutes. Pour reserved marinade over chicken and cook a further 10 minutes or until chicken is tender. Serve hot.

Serves 8

Mango Chicken Delight

CHICKEN BREASTS WITH MANGO AND GREEN PEPPERCORN SAUCE

60 g butter
6 chicken breasts, skin
    removed
1 mango, peeled, seeded
    and quartered
1 cup chicken stock
1 shallot, finely chopped
2 teaspoons green
    peppercorns
1 cup cream
1 teaspoon red currant jelly
½ teaspoon dry mustard
    powder
salt and freshly ground
    pepper, to taste

Heat butter in a pan and brown chicken each side. Lift from pan and reserve. Saute mango allowing the fruit to remain firm. Set aside with chicken and keep warm.

Pour stock into the pan and reduce it to a glaze, stirring continually. Add shallots, peppercorns, cream, red currant jelly, mustard and seasoning. Cook mixture until it thickens and adjust the seasoning. Arrange the chicken and mango on plates, pour the sauce over and serve.

Serves 6

CRUNCHY NUT CHICKEN AND MANGO ROLLUPS

6 chicken breasts, pounded
    flat
2 mangoes, peeled and
    sliced
3 cups flour
salt and freshly ground
    pepper, to taste
2 eggs, lightly beaten
2 cups breadcrumbs
2 cups crushed nuts
125 g butter

Place slices of mango on one half of chicken breast. Roll up, tucking in sides and secure with toothpicks. Season flour with salt and pepper. Dip each chicken breast firstly into the flour, coat well with beaten egg, then dip into breadcrumbs and nuts until well covered. Set aside in refrigerator for a minimum 1½ hours or overnight.

To cook, heat butter in a pan over moderate heat. Saute chicken for 6–7 minutes each side or until golden brown. The chicken is cooked when the juice has no trace of pinkness when pierced with a skewer.

Serves 4

Note: The chicken breasts may be prepared to cooking stage the day before.

BARBECUED CHICKEN WITH MANGO GLAZE

6 chicken breasts, lightly
    pounded
1 tablespoon mango
    chutney
1 teaspoon Worcestershire
    sauce
½ cup mayonnaise
1 tablespoon apricot jam or
    mango jam (see recipe)
2 teaspoons mustard
1 tablespoon lemon juice
salt and pepper, to taste
parsley, to garnish

Place chicken in a dish. Combine chutney, Worcestershire sauce, mayonnaise, apricot jam, mustard and lemon juice. Spoon over the chicken. Marinate for several hours, covered, in a refrigerator.

Barbecue the chicken until well cooked, basting frequently with the marinade to glaze. Season to taste, garnish with parsley and serve hot.

Serves 6

CHICKEN WITH GREEN MANGO CURRY

1.5 kg chicken, jointed
1 green mango, peeled,
    seeded and diced
1 cup chicken stock
½ teaspoon salt
¾ teaspoon turmeric
½ coconut
3 green chillies, seeded
6 cloves garlic, peeled
¼ teaspoon cumin seeds
1 tablespoon ghee or
    clarified butter
½ teaspoon mustard seeds
3 curry leaves

Cook chicken and mango in stock seasoned with salt and ¼ teaspoon turmeric for 45 minutes or until tender.

Grind the coconut, chillies, garlic, ½ teaspoon turmeric and cumin seeds. Add this mixture to chicken and cook 5 minutes. Heat ghee and fry mustard seeds and curry leaves until mustard seeds begin to splutter. Add to curry. Mix well and serve.

Serves 4

From top clockwise: Crunchy Nut Chicken and Mango Rollups; Barbecued Chicken with Mango Glaze; Chicken Breasts with Mango and Green Peppercorn Sauce

PARTRIDGE WITH CREAMY MANGO COULIS

2 partridges or spatchcock
freshly ground pepper, to
    taste
2 rashers bacon
50 g unsalted butter,
    clarified
2 shallots, chopped
1 clove garlic, crushed
1 sheet frozen puff pastry,
    thawed and cut into 4
    triangles
1 mango, peeled, seeded
    and julienned

Creamy Mango Coulis
2 mangoes, peeled, seeded
    and roughly chopped
2 tablespoons cream

Season the partridges, place bacon on top and roast for
30–40 minutes in a preheated oven at 220°C (425°F). When
cooked, remove all flesh from the bone, discarding bacon
and skin. Saute shallots and garlic in butter until tender,
then add chopped meat. Season to taste.

Cook pastry triangles at 200°C (400°F) for 12 minutes or
until golden brown. When cooked, cut horizontally
through triangles to make 2 halves. Pour warmed mango
coulis in the centre of 4 warm plates. Sandwich the partridge mixture between the pastry triangles, and garnish
with mango.

Creamy Mango Coulis: Puree mango and cream
together until smooth. Heat through gently just before
assembling dish.

Serves 4

MARINATED CHICKEN WITH MANGO FRUIT DIP

3 chicken breasts, halved

Marinade
½ cup honey
¼ cup lime juice
¼ cup oil
1 clove garlic, crushed
salt and freshly ground
    pepper, to taste

Mango Fruit Dip
2 mangoes
2 teaspoons lime juice
1 tablespoon honey
¼ cup cream
¼ cup orange juice
curry powder, to taste
salt and freshly ground
    pepper, to taste

Arrange breasts in a shallow baking dish. Combine marinade ingredients, pour over the chicken, cover and marinate 1 hour, turning occasionally.

Drain chicken and place on an oiled grill or barbecue.
Basting frequently with marinade, grill until cooked
through and brown on each side.

Mango Fruit Dip: Puree the mangoes and combine
with remaining ingredients. Cover and refrigerate until
ready to serve.

Serves 6

STIR-FRIED MANGO CHICKEN WITH SHALLOT AND ALMONDS

3 chicken breasts, skinned,
    boned and cut into thin
    strips
6 tablespoons safflower oil
1½ teaspoons chopped
    ginger root
1 clove garlic, crushed
4 shallots, white part
    chopped and green part
    cut into 2.5 cm pieces
salt and freshly ground
    pepper, to taste
2 mangoes, peeled and cut
    in long strips

Marinade
1 tablespoon cornflour
1 tablespoon light soy sauce
2 tablespoons sherry

Sauce
1 tablespoon light soy sauce
2 tablespoons sherry
1 teaspoon brown sugar
1 teaspoon cornflour
shallot tassels to garnish
½ cup slivered almonds,
    toasted

Combine all the ingredients for the marinade. Spoon over
chicken strips, marinate in the refrigerator for 30 minutes
then drain.

Heat 3 tablespoons oil in a wok over high heat, stir-fry
chicken for 30 seconds, remove and drain on absorbent
paper. Heat 2 tablespoons oil and stir-fry ginger, garlic and
white part of the shallots for 30 seconds. Reheat chicken
in the wok, season and stir-fry for 1 minute. Place chicken
in a serving dish.

Heat 1 tablespoon of oil in the wok and add mangoes.
Stir-fry for 30 seconds, then add soy sauce, sherry, sugar
and cornflour. Cook 30 seconds or until the sauce thickens.

Left: Stir-fried Mango Chicken with Shallot and Almonds; right: Marinated Chicken with Mango Fruit Dip

Add the green shallot pieces and toasted almonds. Pour over the chicken and decorate with shallot tassels.

Shallot Tassels: To make shallot tassels, cut into 5 cm lengths. Leaving 1 cm at end uncut, make 6–8 slits along the shallot with a sharp knife, making about 6–8 fronds. Soak in icy water until the fronds curl.

Serves 4

GLAZED MANGO AND WALNUT PORK

1.5 kg pork loin, boned and
  skinned
2 tablespoons walnut oil
1 teaspoon flour
¼ cup orange juice
salt and freshly ground
  pepper, to taste

Stuffing
300 g mango flesh, roughly
  chopped
1 cup walnuts, roughly
  chopped
½ cup breadcrumbs
1 egg
salt and freshly ground
  pepper, to taste
½ cup orange juice

Glaze
½ cup orange juice
2 tablespoons sugar
freshly ground black
  pepper, to taste
walnut or olive oil, to taste

To make stuffing, combine the mango, walnuts, breadcrumbs, egg and seasoning. Pour in enough orange juice to bind the mixture. Refrigerate, covered, overnight.

Spoon stuffing under flap of pork loin, form into an even shape and tie with string every 5 cm. Brush with oil, sprinkle with pepper and cook in an oven preheated to 290°C (550°F) for 10 minutes. Reduce heat to 220°C (425°F) and cook a further 20 minutes.

To make the glaze, combine the orange juice with the sugar. Season with pepper and walnut oil to taste. Brush the glaze over the meat and return to the oven. When a golden crust has formed, remove pork and set aside in a warm place.

Skim fat off pan, add flour and stir, add orange juice and deglaze the pan. Add more juice, water or stock to make up desired quantity and thickness of sauce. Season to taste. Slice the pork, arrange on individual plates and pour over a little of the sauce.

Serves 6–8

MANGO PORK MEDALLIONS

1 teaspoon oil
1 clove garlic, crushed
4 × 150 g pork medallion
  steaks, trimmed of excess
  fat
1 onion, finely sliced
1 tablespoon flaked
  almonds

Mango Sauce
1 cup mango, pureed
cinnamon, to taste
1 tablespoon cream
paprika, to taste
parsley sprigs, to garnish

Heat oil in frying pan and fry garlic until soft. Add pork and cook 2–3 minutes each side or until tender. Set steaks aside and stir-fry onions and almonds. Reserve and keep warm.

Mango Sauce: Heat mango and cinnamon in saucepan, then add cream and adjust seasonings. Spoon over enough sauce to coat each medallion.

Serve pork with the rest of the sauce separately. Sprinkle over paprika and garnish with parsley sprigs.

Serves 4

BUTTERFLY MANGO PORK

60 g butter
2 small onions, finely
  chopped
8 butterfly pork chops, all
  excess fat trimmed
freshly ground pepper, to
  taste
¼ cup flour
1½ cups pineapple juice
¼ cup chicken stock
½ mango, cut into bite-
  sized pieces
1½ tablespoons cornflour
⅓ cup fresh cream
parsley sprigs, to garnish

Melt 10 g butter and fry onions until soft. Drain on absorbent paper. Season pork chops with pepper and dust lightly with flour. Melt remaining butter and fry chops gently until just cooked.

Pour pineapple juice, chicken stock and mango pieces into a saucepan and heat through. Mix cornflour and a little water to a paste-like consistency and add to the mango mixture. Stir until thickened, then take off heat. Stir in cream.

Place pork in a casserole dish and pour over sauce. Cover and bake in an oven preheated to 180°C (350°F) for 15 minutes. Serve garnished with parsley sprigs.

Serves 4

CAMEMBERT MANGO SURPRISE

2 small canned Camembert
    cheeses
4 slices smoked salmon
1 avocado, peeled, seeded
    and sliced
juice 1 lemon
¾ cup flour, seasoned
1 egg, lightly beaten
1½ cups breadcrumbs
½ cup pecan nuts, finely
    chopped
oil for deep-frying
½ lime, cut into 4 thin slices
watercress sprigs, to
    garnish

Coulis
1 mango, peeled, seeded
    and pureed or
    425 g can mango slices,
    drained and pureed with
    juice ½ lime

Halve each Camembert horizontally. On 2 halves, place smoked salmon and three-quarters of avocado slices sprinkled with lemon juice. Replace tops and press together firmly.

Dip each Camembert round first in flour, then in egg, then in breadcrumbs and nuts and chill. For a firmer crust, repeat process.

Heat the oil and deep-fry cheese until crust is golden brown. Drain on absorbent paper then cook in an oven preheated to 180°C (350°F) for 10–15 minutes.

Spoon mango coulis on each serving plate and place a Camembert in the middle. Garnish with remaining avocado slices (sprinkled with lemon juice), lime slices and watercress sprigs.

Serves 2

MANGO PROSCUITTO

250 g proscuitto, thinly
    sliced
1 mango, peeled, seeded
    and sliced
4 pears, peeled and sliced
2 kiwi fruit, peeled and
    sliced
creamed cottage cheese, to
    serve

Arrange slices of proscuitto and fruits alternately on a large serving platter or 4 individual plates. Serve with creamed cottage cheese.

Serves 4

SPICY HAM AND MANGO BAKE

1 tablespoon oil
1 onion, finely sliced
450 g leg ham, sliced into
    1 cm thick slices
1 teaspoon fenugreek
1 clove garlic, crushed
½ teaspoon cumin
¼ cup white wine
1 tablespoon mango
    chutney
2 teaspoons cornflour
¾ cup water
1 mango, peeled, seeded
    and sliced thinly
½ red capsicum, finely
    sliced
½ green capsicum, finely
    sliced

Heat oil in a pan, add onion and fry until tender. Place in an ovenproof dish and lay slices of ham over onions.

Fry garlic, fenugreek and cumin for 1 minute in pan then add wine and chutney. Blend the cornflour with a little of the water, then add remaining water. Pour this into pan and stir until sauce boils and thickens. Cover and simmer for 5 minutes.

Pour sauce over ham and onions, top with mango and capsicum. Bake in an oven preheated to 180°C (350°F) for 10 minutes or until heated through.

Serves 4

Something for the Family

W hat does the harassed cook do to tickle the family's tastebuds without creating dishes which are too different, too time consuming, or too costly for the everyday budget?

The answer comes in the shape of the mango. Its tangy and distinctive flavour gives an imaginative accent to otherwise traditional family fare, but is not such a radical departure from regular dishes that picky eaters will complain.

Eggs with Prawns and Mango

VEAL WITH FRESH MANGO SLICES

500 g thin veal steaks,
*   membrane removed to*
*   prevent shrinkage*
2 tablespoons flour
salt and freshly ground
*   pepper, to taste*
1 tablespoon oil
20 g butter
2 tablespoons Grand
*   Marnier*
½ cup chicken stock
½ cup white wine
1 teaspoon wholegrain
*   mustard*
lemon juice
2 tablespoons cream
2 mangoes, peeled and
*   sliced*

Coat veal in seasoned flour. Reserve remaining flour. Heat oil and butter in a pan, and fry veal each side on high heat for 2 minutes. Add Grand Marnier and simmer 1 minute. Remove veal and keep warm.

Place pan over heat and evaporate moisture until only fat is left; pour off leaving only 1 tablespoon in pan. Add remaining flour and cook 1 minute, then add stock and wine stirring constantly until sauce thickens. Stir in mustard, lemon juice, cream and mango slices and heat gently, adjusting seasoning if necessary. Arrange mangoes on the veal and spoon the sauce over.

Serves 4

SPICY MEATBALLS WITH MANGO YOGHURT SAUCE

1 kg beef, finely minced
2 onions, finely chopped
2 tablespoons chopped
*   mint*
1½ cups soft white
*   breadcrumbs*
3 eggs, lightly beaten
3 tablespoons oil
3 tablespoons lemon juice
3 cloves garlic, crushed
½ teaspoon nutmeg
salt and freshly ground
*   pepper, to taste*
oil, for frying

Mango Yoghurt Sauce
2 cups natural yoghurt
2 tablespoons mango
*   chutney*
½ teaspoon curry powder

Combine meat, onions, mint, breadcrumbs, eggs, oil, lemon juice, garlic, nutmeg, salt and pepper. Roll into walnut-sized balls with wetted hands. Heat about 2 cm depth of oil in a pan and cook meatballs, one layer at a time. Drain and keep warm.

Mango Yoghurt Sauce: Combine all the ingredients for sauce and serve separately in a bowl with the meatballs.

Makes about 40

STIR-FRIED BEEF WITH HAM AND MANGO

2 tablespoons oil
1 onion, cut into segments
375 g rump or topside
*   steak, cut into strips*
425 g can mango slices,
*   drained and cut into*
*   strips, juice reserved*
1 tablespoon soy sauce
2 tablespoons tomato sauce
1 tablespoon cornflour
1 tablespoon sugar
375 g ham steaks, julienned
½ green capsicum, seeded
*   and finely sliced*

Heat oil in a pan, add onion and meat and stir-fry until brown. Drain off fat. Pour in mango juice with the soy sauce. Cover and simmer for 20 minutes or until tender.

Blend the tomato sauce with cornflour and brown sugar in pan and stir until boiling gently and sauce has thickened. Add ham and capsicum and simmer for 5 minutes, then stir in mango strips to warm through. Adjust seasonings and serve.

Serves 4–6

BEEF WITH MANGO MARINADE

6 fillet steaks

Marinade
½ cup mango juice
1 teaspoon cinnamon
1 tablespoon finely
*   chopped onion*
1 teaspoon chilli and garlic
*   sauce*
parsley, to garnish

Combine marinade ingredients in a dish and coat each side of beef steaks. Stand, covered for 1 hour or leave in refrigerator overnight. Cook under a medium-hot grill or on barbecue for 5 minutes each side or until cooked to taste. Brush with marinade while cooking. Serve garnished with parsley accompanied by fresh salad.

Serves 6

From top clockwise: Stir-fried Beef with Ham and Mango; Veal with Fresh Mango Slices; Spicy Meatballs with Mango Yoghurt Sauce

RACKS OF LAMB WITH PARSLEY MINT CRUST

60 g butter
1 tablespoon mango
    chutney
2 teaspoons French
    mustard
1 clove garlic, crushed
2 teaspoons lemon juice
6 racks lamb (4 chops each),
    excess fat trimmed
¾ cup finely chopped
    parsley
¼ cup finely chopped mint
salt and freshly ground
    pepper, to taste
2 mangoes, peeled, seeded
    and sliced

Mango Mint Sauce
1 mango, peeled, seeded
    and pureed
1 tablespoon finely
    chopped fresh mint
freshly ground pepper, to
    taste
1 teaspoon vinegar

Combine butter, chutney, mustard, garlic and lemon juice. Spread evenly over the back of each lamb rack. Sprinkle over parsley and mint, and press onto lamb using the back of a metal spoon. Season well with salt and pepper and cook in an oven preheated to 200° (400°F) for 20–30 minutes or until tender. Serve with Mango Mint Sauce.
Mango Mint Sauce: Combine ingredients for sauce in a small saucepan. Heat gently then serve.
    Serves 6

MANGO TOPPED LAMB CHOPS

8 lamb loin chops
salt and freshly ground
    pepper, to taste
½ cup finely chopped
    parsley
2 mangoes peeled, seeded
    and diced
½ teaspoon cinnamon

Preheat the grill to high. Season the chops with salt and pepper and grill each side for 6–8 minutes depending on thickness.
    Remove from the grill just before they are cooked.
    Sprinkle parsley evenly over chops, then arrange the mango slices on top. Sprinkle with cinnamon and place under grill again. Cook until the mango browns slightly.
    Serves 4

Above: Mango Topped Lamb Chops;
below: Rack of Lamb with Parsley Mint
Crust

SHOULDER OF LAMB WITH MANGO AND PAWPAW SAUCE

1 kg shoulder young lamb
salt and freshly ground
    pepper, to taste
80 g butter
1 teaspoon allspice
2 tablespoons honey
1 pawpaw, seeded
425 g can mango slices,
    juice reserved
parsley sprigs, to garnish

Season lamb with salt and pepper, cover with butter and place in a roasting pan. Roast the meat in an oven preheated to 200°C (400°F) for 30 minutes, then reduce the temperature to 180°C (350°F) and cook for a further 30 minutes. Combine the allspice with honey and baste the meat while cooking.

Scoop out the pawpaw into balls with a melon baller. Add the mango slices and pawpaw balls to the pan 15 minutes before the end of roasting. When cooked, transfer the meat to a warm dish and surround it with mango and pawpaw.

Drain off all excess fat, then use a little of the canned juice to loosen the browned sediment in the roasting pan. Boil, season, strain and serve separately. Garnish the dish with sprigs of parsley and serve.

Serves 4

ROAST PORK WITH WARMED MANGO SLICES

1.5 kg pork shoulder
1 clove garlic, crushed
1 teaspoon honey
1 teaspoon curry powder
rind 1 orange
1 teaspoon salt
425 g can mango slices,
    juice reserved and
    mangoes chopped
freshly ground pepper, to
    taste
½ cup orange juice
1 tablespoon cornflour

Score the pork rind lightly and make a few incisions with knife between the rind. Blend together garlic, honey, curry powder, orange rind and spoon into these incisions between rind. Rub salt over rind. Place pork on a rack in a baking pan then season with pepper. Bake in oven preheated to 220°C (420°F) for 30 minutes. Reduce the heat and continue to cook at 180°C (350°F) for 1¼ hours. Remove pork and keep warm.

Pour off all excess fat. Combine cooking juices and mango juice with orange juice blended with cornflour and stir until the sauce boils and thickens. Add mango pieces and warm through. Adjust seasonings and serve with sliced pork.

Serves 6–8

MEDITERRANEAN BEEF WITH CINNAMON MANGOES

2 fillet steaks
salt and freshly ground
    pepper, to taste
paprika, to taste
425 g can mango slices,
    juice reserved
1 tablespoon brown sugar
¼ cup dates, seeded and
    finely chopped
¼ teaspoon cinnamon
1 clove
2 teaspoons cornflour,
    dissolved in 3 teaspoons
    water

Season steaks with salt, pepper and paprika. Grill for 5 minutes on each side.

Puree mango juice and slices and simmer in saucepan with sugar, dates, cinnamon and clove for 5 minutes. Add dissolved cornflour and cook, stirring constantly until it thickens. Remove clove and serve with the steaks.

Serves 2

SAUCY FRUIT PORK PARCELS

	Sauce
8 pork steaks or schnitzels	1½ cups chicken stock
⅔ cup fruit chutney	1 tablespoon tomato paste
⅓ cup dry breadcrumbs	3 teaspoons soy sauce
1 shallot, chopped	1 tablespoon cornflour
1 fresh mango, peeled and	freshly ground pepper, to
seeded	taste
1 tablespoon oil	
20 g butter	

Flatten pork with a meat mallet until very thin. Combine chutney, breadcrumbs and shallot and spread over pork steaks. Place a thick slice of mango at one end and roll up pork slice firmly. Tie with cotton to make a parcel.

Heat oil and butter in a pan and brown pork evenly for 7 minutes turning frequently.

Sauce: Blend all sauce ingredients, then add to pan. Reduce heat to medium-low and stir until thickened. Cover and simmer very slowly for 35 minutes or until pork is tender, turning often. Remove cotton and serve.

Serves 6–8

Saucy Fruit Pork Parcels

1   Flatten pork with meat mallet until very thin

2   Spread chutney, shallot and breadcrumb mixture on steaks

3   Place a thick slice of mango at one end

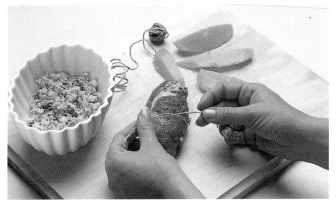

4   Tie with cotton to make parcel

SAGE PORK AND MANGO

2 pork steaks (about 200 g
    each)
¼ teaspoon sage
salt and freshly ground
    pepper, to taste
1 tablespoon oil
3 teaspoons white vinegar
¾ cup chicken stock
425 g can mango slices,
    juice reserved and
    mango julienned
1 tablespoon cornflour

Season pork steaks with sage, salt and pepper. Heat oil in pan and brown steaks both sides. Reduce heat and cook for about 10 minutes then transfer to plate and keep warm.

Add vinegar and stock to pan and bring to boil, stirring. Reduce heat. Add mango juice combined with cornflour and stir until thickened. Return steaks to pan and stir in the mango. Simmer gently for 2 minutes. Adjust seasonings, then serve.

Serves 2

HAM STEAKS WITH CURRIED MANGO SAUCE

4 ham steaks
1 tablespoon oil

Curried Mango Sauce
1½ cups orange and mango
    juice
2 tablespoons cornflour
1 teaspoon curry powder
½ teaspoon cinnamon
¼ cup white wine
½ cup mango, peeled,
    seeded and sliced
½ cup banana, peeled and
    sliced
½ cup sultana grapes

Heat juice in pan on medium heat. Meanwhile, blend together cornflour, curry powder and cinnamon with wine. Add to pan and stir until thickened. Simmer for 3 minutes, then add fruit to sauce and simmer for 1 minute more.

Heat oil in pan, add ham steaks and cook for 3 minutes or until brown on both sides. Serve ham steaks with sauce poured over.

Serves 4

EGGS WITH PRAWNS AND MANGO

8 eggs, hard-boiled and
    shelled
60 g butter
1 onion, finely chopped
1 cooking apple, peeled and
    finely chopped
2 teaspoons curry powder
2 tablespoons flour
1½ cups chicken stock
1 mango, peeled, seeded
    and sliced
3 tablespoons mango
    chutney, chopped
1 tablespoon lemon juice
salt and freshly ground
    pepper, to taste
500 g prawns, peeled
2 tablespoons finely
    chopped parsley, to
    garnish

Cut eggs in half lengthways and place, cut side down, in an ovenproof serving dish. Keep warm while cooking the sauce.

In a pan, melt butter and fry onion and apple until soft. Add curry powder and cook for a minute, then add flour and stir in. Gradually add the stock; bring to boil and simmer 2 minutes. Add mango, chutney, lemon juice, salt, pepper and prawns. Simmer 3 minutes then spoon mixture over eggs and garnish with parsley.

Serves 6–8

HAM STEAKS WITH MAPLE MANGO SAUCE

4 ham steaks, about 125 g
    each

Maple Mango Sauce
40 g butter
4 slices mango
2 tablespoons cornflour
¾ cup orange and mango
    juice
⅓ cup finely sliced shallots
¼ red capsicum, seeded
    and cut into strips
1 tablespoon maple syrup

To make sauce, melt 20 g butter in pan over medium heat. Add cornflour and blend in juice. Bring to boil and stir until sauce thickens. Add shallots, capsicum and maple syrup, and simmer for 3 minutes on low heat. Remove from pan and keep warm.

Melt remaining butter in pan and quickly brown ham steaks then stir in mango slices. Serve steaks topped with sauce.

Serves 4

MANGO PILAF

2 cups long-grain rice
1 teaspoon salt
½ teaspoon turmeric
1 teaspoon cumin seeds
6 red chillies, seeded and
    chopped
2 cups grated coconut
6 half-ripe mangoes, peeled
    and chopped
125 g ghee or clarified
    butter
3–4 curry leaves
2 teaspoons mustard seeds
2 whole red chillies, to
    garnish

Boil rice with salt and turmeric until cooked. While rice is cooking, grind together cumin seeds, 3 chillies and coconut. Mix with mangoes. Add to cooked rice with half the ghee. Set aside.

Heat remaining ghee and fry curry leaves, mustard seeds and 3 chillies until mustard seeds start to pop. Combine with rice mixture. Serve garnished with whole red chillies.

Serves 6

SPICED CHICKEN AND MANGO CURRY

2 tablespoons oil
6 chicken fillets, cut into
    bite-size pieces
1 clove garlic, crushed
1 medium-sized onion,
    chopped
1½ teaspoons curry
    powder
1 teaspoon chillies
¼ teaspoon turmeric
¼ teaspoon cinnamon
½ cup coconut milk
½ cup chicken stock
salt and freshly ground
    pepper, to taste
1 mango, peeled, seeded
    and cut into 3 cm pieces
90 g roasted, unsalted
    cashew nuts

Heat oil in frypan and fry chicken pieces until brown and almost cooked. Remove from pan and drain on absorbent paper. Add garlic and onion to the pan and cook until soft. Stir in curry powder, ground chillies, turmeric and cinnamon. Cook for 2 minutes. Pour in coconut milk and stock to pan and stir until boiling. Season to taste with salt and pepper.

Return chicken to pan and cook gently for 3 minutes. Add mango pieces and cashew nuts and heat through gently.

Serves 4–6

MANGO CHICKEN GINGER

4 chicken fillets
3 tablespoons seasoned
    flour
1 tablespoon oil
40 g butter
2 mangoes, peeled, seeded
    and sliced
2 teaspoons finely chopped
    preserved ginger
1 tablespoon French
    mustard
¼ teaspoon dried tarragon
1 tablespoon honey
1 cup dry white wine
½ cup cream
salt and freshly ground
    pepper, to taste

Garnish
1 mango, peeled, seeded
    and sliced
½ green capsicum, finely
    sliced
12 black olives

Dust chicken fillets in flour and pan fry in hot oil and butter until golden brown on both sides. Add mango slices, cover and simmer for 5 minutes. Stir in ginger, mustard, tarragon, honey and wine. Return to boil, cover and simmer for 2 minutes. Lift out chicken and keep warm.

Puree mango sauce until smooth, then return to pan and stir in cream. Season to taste. Serve garnished with mango slices, black olives and capsicum strips.

Serves 6–8

CHICKEN AND MANGO IN TARRAGON WINE SAUCE

60 g butter
4 chicken breasts
½ onion, finely chopped
4 tablespoons tarragon
    vinegar
⅓ cup chicken stock
1 tablespoon white wine
⅓ cup cream
2 mangoes, peeled, seeded
    and pureed
salt and freshly ground
    pepper, to taste
½ mango, peeled, seeded
    and sliced, to garnish
tarragon sprigs, to garnish

Melt butter in pan and brown chicken for about 4 minutes each side until lightly browned then set aside. Add onion to pan and cook on low heat for 5 minutes, then add tarragon vinegar. Increase heat and cook until sauce is reduced to a syrup. Add stock and wine, then stir in cream and mango puree. Season to taste, stirring for 2 minutes. Strain sauce and return to pan. Add chicken and reheat. Serve garnished with mango slices and fresh tarragon sprigs.

Serves 4

CHICKEN AND MANGO RISOTTO

50 g butter
4 tablespoons seasoned
    flour
1.5 kg chicken, jointed or
    chicken pieces
1 large onion, thinly sliced
pinch nutmeg
juice and finely grated rind
    ½ lemon
⅔ cup chicken stock
salt and freshly ground
    pepper, to taste
2 mangoes, peeled, seeded
    and sliced
⅔ cup cream
½ red capsicum, finely
    sliced, for garnish

Risotto
50 g butter
1 small onion, finely
    chopped
1½ cups long-grain rice,
    rinsed until water is clear
2½ cups chicken stock
salt and freshly ground
    pepper, to taste
1 teaspoon turmeric

Heat butter in a large, heavy-based saucepan. Toss chicken in seasoned flour until evenly coated. Gently fry chicken pieces and onion until golden brown. Drain on absorbent paper, then place into a casserole dish. Add nutmeg, lemon rind, stock and seasoning and pour over chicken. Cover and cook in an oven preheated to 180°C (350°F) for 45 minutes. Add mango slices and cook a further 15 minutes. When chicken is tender, remove pieces from casserole and keep warm.

Bring sauce to boil, adding lemon juice to taste. Stir in cream and cook until sauce thickens slightly. Adjust seasonings to taste.

Place chicken on a serving dish and pour sauce over. Garnish with capsicum strips.

Risotto: Heat butter in a saucepan and fry onion until transparent. Add rice and stir-fry for 5 minutes over low heat. Pour in stock, stirring well and bring to the boil. Season to taste, turn heat down low, cover and simmer rice for 20 minutes or until all stock has been absorbed. Do not stir or remove lid during this time. Fluff rice gently with a fork and stir in turmeric until all the rice is coated with yellow. Serve separately with chicken.

Serves 4

Left: Chicken and Mango in Tarragon Wine Sauce; right: Chicken and Mango Risotto

Something Tempting

The temptation of the mango is that it makes a delicious dessert whether served as a complicated confection or simply presented as deliciously fresh fruit.

It is endlessly versatile. Mango can be pulped, pureed, baked, stewed, marinated — the possibilities are limitless. Try it in a tart, pureed in a fool, or simply served in slim slices.

From top right clockwise: Mango Lime Custard; Chilled Ginger Mango Souffle; Mango Charlotte

FRESH FRUIT TART

Crust
250 g Granita biscuits
125 g butter, melted

Custard
½ cup custard powder
½ cup water
2 × 400 g cans condensed
    milk
2 cups warm water
2 eggs, lightly beaten
½ cup Tia Maria
½ cup desiccated coconut
1½ cups whipped cream
mangoes, lychees, cherries,
    to decorate

Crumb the biscuits. Melt the butter and add to the crumbs. Press crumb mixture onto base and sides of 21 cm spring-form tin. Refrigerate until firm.

Place the custard powder and ½ cup water into a saucepan and mix well. Stir in the condensed milk. Add the warm water and the lightly beaten egg. Stir constantly over low heat until the custard boils. Cook until the mixture is very thick. Remove from heat and beat vigorously with a wooden spoon until smooth. Cool, then add the Tia Maria and coconut.

Fold the whipped cream into the custard mixture. Spoon mixture into the chilled crust. Chill for 1–2 hours and then top with fresh fruit. Serve with extra whipped cream.

Serves 4

MANGO TART

1 cup flour, sifted
pinch salt
60 g butter, softened
⅓ cup caster sugar
2 egg yolks
2 drops vanilla

Filling
½ cup peeled and finely
    chopped banana
⅓ cup finely chopped
    walnuts
1 cup vanilla ice cream,
    softened
small mangoes, peeled,
    seeded and sliced into
    quarters
juice ½ lemon
300 mL cream, whipped
1 mango, peeled and sliced,
    for serving or 450 g can
    mango slices
½ teaspoon nutmeg

Sift flour and salt into a work surface, making a well in the centre. Place remaining ingredients in the well and quickly mix them together using the fingertips of one hand. Gradually incorporate all the flour and mix to form a smooth dough. Knead on a lightly floured surface for 1–2 minutes. Wrap in plastic wrap and chill for 1 hour before using.

Roll the pastry out on a lightly floured board to fit a 20 cm flan tin. Prick base with a fork. Bake blind in an oven preheated to 210°C (400°F) for 20–25 minutes or until a light golden colour. Allow to cool.

Filling: Mix together banana, walnuts and ice cream and spoon into pastry shell. Chill for 15 minutes. Spoon cream into centre of tart and top with mango. Serve chilled.

Serves 4

SUMMERTIME TART

Pastry
125 g butter, softened
½ cup caster sugar
1¼ cups flour, sifted
⅓ cup cocoa
1 egg, beaten

Filling
3 eggs, beaten
⅓ cup caster sugar
3 mangoes, peeled, seeded
*   and pureed or 3 × 450 g*
*   cans mango slices*
375 g fresh ricotta cheese
3 tablespoons Kirsch

Garnish
1 mango, peeled, seeded
*   and sliced*
⅓ cup passionfruit pulp

Cream butter and sugar until light and fluffy, add the dry ingredients and blend the egg well into the mixture. Knead lightly, wrap in plastic wrap and refrigerate for 30 minutes. Roll out pastry to a 27 cm flan tin. Prick base with fork and bake blind in an oven preheated to 180°C (350°F) for 10 minutes.

Filling: Blend together eggs, sugar, mangoes, ricotta and Kirsch. Pour into cooled pastry shell. Bake for 35 minutes at 180°C (350°F); cool.

Arrange mango slices decoratively on tart and spoon over passionfruit. Serve with fresh cream.

Serves 8

Note: This tart is best eaten the day that it is made.

FRESH FRUIT SHORTCAKE

120 g butter
4 tablespoons sugar
4 egg yolks
1½ cups flour

Topping
2½ cups cream, whipped
2 cups chopped fruit
*   (mangoes, nectarines and*
*   apricots)*
2 nectarines, halved,
*   seeded and finely sliced*

Cream butter and sugar until light and fluffy. Add egg yolks one at a time and beat well after each addition. Sift flour and mix until well combined. Knead dough on lightly floured working surface. Place on greased pizza tray and, using your knuckles or fingertips, press out to fit tray. Bake blind in an oven preheated to 180°C (350°F) for 20–25 minutes or until lightly browned. Remove from oven and, when cold, gently lift shortcake onto serving dish.

Topping: Combine cream and fruit and spoon onto shortcake base. Arrange nectarine slices on cream with skin-side showing. Serve slightly chilled.

Serves 10–12

Note: The shortcake base may be cooked up to 2 days ahead of time and stored in a covered container.

Left to right: Summertime Tart,
Fresh Fruit Tart, Mango Tart

GINGER MANGO CHEESECAKE

Crust
125 g butter, melted
2½ cups chocolate biscuit
 crumbs

Filling
¼ cup boiling water
¼ cup lemon juice
25 g packet lemon jelly
 crystals
375 g can evaporated milk,
 chilled
200 g soft cream cheese
2 mangoes, peeled, seeded
 and roughly chopped or
 2 × 450 g cans mango
 slices
¼ cup brown sugar
vanilla essence, to taste
1 tablespoon glace ginger,
 finely chopped

Garnish
1 mango, sliced
whipped cream
½ lemon, thinly sliced and
 cut into small pieces
chocolate curls

Combine melted butter and biscuit crumbs thoroughly. Flatten across the bottom and sides of a greased 23 cm spring-form pan and chill.

Filling: Heat water and lemon juice until boiling, add jelly crystals and stir to dissolve. Allow to cool. Whip evaporated milk until thick, add cream cheese and mangoes then beat until smooth. Add sugar, vanilla essence, ginger and jelly mixture. Pour over crumb crust and chill.

Decorate with mango slices, piped cream, lemon pieces and chocolate curls.

Serves 10–12

MANGO CREAM CREPES

1 cup self-raising flour
1 tablespoon caster sugar
1 egg
¾–1 cup buttermilk
1 apple, grated
2 bananas, peeled and diced
2 mangoes, peeled, seeded
 and chopped
300 mL cream, whipped
2 tablespoons icing sugar

Sift flour and sugar into a bowl. Lightly beat egg and make up to 1 cup with buttermilk. Gradually pour into flour and mix until smooth. Add grated apple.

Drop large spoonfuls of batter into a hot, lightly greased non-stick frypan. Flatten crepes out slightly. When bubbles appear on the top, turn crepes over and cook until browned.

Sprinkle banana with lemon juice. Combine the mangoes and bananas and spread fruit and cream mixture on crepes. Fold in half. Serve with a dusting of icing sugar.

From bottom clockwise: Ginger Mango
Cheesecake; Mango Cream Crepes;
Fresh Fruit Shortcake

1   Line a 23 cm spring-form pan with foil

2   Spoon butter and breadcrumb mixture into tin

3   Flatten sides and base using a glass

4   Prick base with a fork

MANGO CREPES WITH SWEET WINE SAUCE

Crepe Batter
½ cup flour
salt, to taste
2 eggs, lightly beaten
¾ cup milk
1 teaspoon brandy
20 g butter

Filling
2 mangoes, peeled, seeded
    and sliced

Sauce
1½ cups sauterne or sweet
    wine
½ cup brown sugar
rind ½ orange
5 cm piece cinnamon stick

To make the crepe batter, sift dry ingredients into bowl, add eggs and stir until mixture is smooth. Gradually add milk and brandy. Leave to stand, covered, in refrigerator for at least 30 minutes before cooking.

Heat crepe pan and grease lightly with butter. When butter turns a golden brown, pour 1½ tablespoons crepe batter into heated pan. Swirl mixture around pan to make an even crepe. Cook on medium heat until light brown. Turn pancake and cook other side. Repeat with remaining batter. Stack crepes and keep warm.

Place mango slices into warm crepes and roll up or fold into triangles. Arrange on serving plates and pour over warm sauce.

Sauce: Put sauterne, sugar, orange and cinnamon in a saucepan, bring to the boil and reduce by half. Strain and keep warm.

Serves 4

MANGO MILLE FEUILLE

3 sheets frozen puff pastry,
    thawed
½ cup icing sugar, sifted
4 tablespoons mango or
    apricot jam
1 mango, peeled, seeded
    and diced
1 cup cream, whipped
2 kiwi fruit, peeled and
    diced

Dust 2 pastry sheets with ¼ cup icing sugar and prick all over with a fork. Using a pastry cutter, cut out small leaves from the third sheet for decoration. Place all the pastry on oven trays and cook in an oven preheated to 230°C (440°F) until golden brown. Allow to cool. Trim edges to make pastry sheets square and even. Spread 2 layers with jam.

Fold mango pieces through half the cream. Spread mango cream over jam covered sheet. Top with second jam covered sheet and cover with kiwi fruit. Place pastry leaves on top of the kiwi fruit and dust with remaining icing sugar.

Serves 4–6

MANGO ECLAIRS

Eclairs can be made in advance and placed in airtight containers. Fill and top with chocolate only a couple of hours before serving.

Choux Pastry
280 mL water
125 g butter
½ tablespoon sugar
1¼ cups flour
4 eggs, lightly beaten

Filling
125 g chocolate
20 g copha
1 mango, chopped
300 mL cream, whipped

To make pastry, place water, butter and sugar in a saucepan and heat until butter has melted. Remove from heat and add flour, beating rapidly with wooden spoon. Return to heat and beat until mixture forms a soft ball and leaves the side of the pan. Remove from heat and allow to cool for approximately 2 minutes. Gradually add the eggs beating continuously. After all egg has been added, beat for another minute.

Spoon dough into piping bag fitted with either plain or star pipe nozzle. Pipe pastry onto greased scone trays, making eclairs approximately 6 cm in length. Cook in an oven preheated to 250°C (500°F) for approximately 20 minutes or until risen and golden. Transfer to a cooling rack. Cut eclairs in half.

Filling: Melt chocolate and copha over hot water and combine. Turn eclairs upside down and dip top halves of eclairs into chocolate. Leave until dry. Place chopped mango pieces into eclair. Spoon whipped cream into piping bag and pipe into eclair. Replace lids.

Makes 15–20

MANGO BROWN BETTY

60 g butter
1 cup grated fresh coconut
2 cups sliced half-ripe
   mango
¾ cup brown sugar
1 teaspoon cinnamon
3 tablespoons coconut juice

Lime Sauce
1 tablespoon cornflour
½ cup sugar
¼ cup cold water
¾ cup boiling water
40 g butter
2½ tablespoons lime juice

Melt butter and mix with coconut. Place a layer of coconut in a greased medium-sized ovenproof dish then add a layer of mangoes. Mix sugar and cinnamon together and sprinkle over mangoes. Repeat layers ending with coconut. Spoon over coconut juice. Bake in an oven preheated to 180°C (350°F) for 1 hour or until mangoes are soft.
Lime Sauce: Meanwhile, combine cornflour and sugar and mix to a paste with cold water. Gradually stir mixture into boiling water, stirring continuously until thickened. Add butter and lime juice and mix well. Serve over mango.
   Serves 6

MANGO MUNCH

65 g rolled oats
2 tablespoons chopped
   walnuts
2 tablespoons desiccated
   coconut
2 tablespoons wheatgerm
1 tablespoon sesame seeds
1 tablespoon brown sugar
½ teaspoon cinnamon
salt, to taste
2 tablespoons honey
2 tablespoons oil
few drops vanilla essence
3 tablespoons seedless raisins
2 mangoes peeled and seeded
2 bananas, peeled
1½ cups natural yoghurt
2 tablespoons orange juice

Mix together oats, walnuts, coconut, wheatgerm, sesame seeds, sugar, cinnamon and salt.
   Melt honey, oil and vanilla in a pan and stir into the oats mixture. Transfer to a shallow cake tin and bake in an oven preheated to 140°C (275°F) for about 40 minutes until golden, stirring occasionally.
   Add raisins to mixture and leave to cool, without stirring. When cold, crumble it into little chunks.
   Slice mangoes and bananas and mix with yoghurt and orange juice. Sprinkle with the oat mixture and serve.
   Serves 6

MANGO SOUFFLE

1 large mango, peeled,
   seeded and pureed
½ cup caster sugar
1 teaspoon lemon juice
2 tablespoons desiccated
   coconut
5 egg whites
2 tablespoons icing sugar,
   sifted
1 mango, peeled, seeded
   and pureed

Puree mango and 3 tablespoons sugar together, then add lemon juice. Grease a 1.5 litre souffle dish and sprinkle it with coconut.
   Whip the egg whites and sugar, beating until stiff peaks form. Stir a little into the mango puree, then very lightly fold all the puree into the remaining egg white mixture.
   Spoon the souffle into the prepared dish. Run a butter knife around the outside of souffle, 2 cm in from the edge so that the souffle will rise well.
   Bake in an oven preheated to 180°C (350°F) for 30–35 minutes or until puffed and light brown. The centre of the souffle will be slightly concave. Sprinkle the top with icing sugar and serve immediately.
   Serves 4
Note: A sauce made from fresh mango pureed is an excellent accompaniment.

CREAMY MANGO MOUSSE

2 medium-sized mangoes,
   peeled and sliced
2 tablespoons caster sugar
1 tablespoon gelatine
3 tablespoons orange juice
300 mL cream

Garnish
extra cream, whipped
grated chocolate

Puree the mango to make 2 cups. Add sugar to the pulp and mix well.
   Sprinkle gelatine over orange juice and place over hot water to dissolve. Fold dissolved gelatine and juice through mango pulp.
   Whip cream until soft peaks form, then fold through mango mixture. Pour into individual mousse dishes. Refrigerate until firm. Decorate with whipped cream and grated chocolate.
   Serves 6
Note: Canned mangoes can also be used in this recipe.

Mango Chocolate Cups

1 Gently melt chocolate, stirring occasionally

2 Spread chocolate evenly around tin

3 When solid, lift from tins carefully

SUMMER FRUIT MERINGUE

4 egg whites
1 cup caster sugar
1 mango, peeled, seeded
    and sliced
2 kiwi fruit, peeled and
    sliced

Mango Sauce	Kiwi Fruit Sauce
1 mango, peeled, seeded and pureed	3 kiwi fruit, peeled and pureed
1 tablespoon icing sugar	1 tablespoon icing sugar
juice ½ lime	juice ½ lemon

Whisk egg whites until stiff, add caster sugar and whisk until dissolved. Line a baking tray with aluminium foil and spoon meringue into the middle. Smooth meringue with a spatula to make a 22 cm diameter circle. Using fork, fluff the sides to give an uneven texture, leaving a hollow in the middle. Cook in an oven preheated to 120°C (240°F) for 1¼ hours. Allow to cool in the oven with the door ajar. Peel away aluminium foil.

Mango Sauce: Puree mangoes with icing sugar and lime juice. Chill thoroughly.

Kiwi Fruit Sauce: Treat kiwi fruit in the same way, first passing through sieve to remove black seeds; chill well.

Spoon Mango Sauce on half a 25 cm serving plate (with sides). Spoon the Kiwi Fruit Sauce onto the other half. Place the meringue shell on top of sauce and fill the hollow with fruit. Place mango slices on the same side as the Kiwi Fruit Sauce and the kiwi fruit slices on the Mango Sauce Side. Dust with icing sugar and serve.

Serves 8

MANGO CHOCOLATE CUPS

300 g dark chocolate,
    melted
2 medium-sized mangoes,
    peeled, seeded and
    roughly chopped
juice 1 large lime
⅔ cup natural yoghurt
1 teaspoon gelatine
2 teaspoons cold water
4 mint sprigs, to garnish

Light brush 4 × 10 cm individual tart tins with oil. Spoon 2 tablespoons melted chocolate into bottom of each. Using a pastry brush, spread chocolate evenly around the base and sides of tin. Allow to set in refrigerator. Brush with extra chocolate if the cases are too thin. When solid, lift from tins carefully, so as not to break edges.

Puree mango, lime juice and yoghurt. Soften gelatine in cold water, then stir over a bowl of hot water until dissolved. Mix thoroughly with mango mixture. Spoon into individual chocolate cases and chill for at least 2 hours before serving. Garnish with mint leaves.

Serves 4

Above: Mango Chocolate Cups;
below: Summer Fruit Meringue

MANGO LIME CUSTARD

3 egg yolks
½ cup caster sugar
1 tablespoon gelatine
3 tablespoons hot water
juice and grated rind,
    1 large lime
1 mango, peeled, seeded
    and pureed
⅔ cup thickened cream
3 egg whites

Beat egg yolks and sugar in top part of double boiler, until sugar has dissolved and mixture becomes light, creamy and thick. Remove from heat and set aside.

Dissolve gelatine in hot water and add to the mixture. Add lime juice, grated rind, mango puree and cream.

In a separate bowl, whisk egg whites to form soft peaks and gently fold through mango mixture. Leave to set 2 hours. Garnish with fresh unsweetened cream and mango slices.

Serves 4–6
Note: Canned mangoes can also be used in this recipe.

CHILLED GINGER MANGO SOUFFLE

1 mango, peeled, seeded
    and pureed
½ cup apricot nectar
½ cup cream
5 teaspoons gelatine
½ cup cold water
3 egg whites
3 tablespoons caster sugar
1 cup whipped cream
1 tablespoon finely
    chopped glace ginger
4 mint sprigs, to decorate

Combine mango puree, apricot nectar and cream. In a small bowl, sprinkle gelatine over cold water and leave 5 minutes to soften. Stand bowl in a pan of simmering water to dissolve gelatine.

Combine gelatine and mango mixture, then chill until mixture becomes thick but not set.

Whisk egg whites until soft peaks form, add sugar and whisk until stiff. Fold in gelatine mixture and pour into 4 individual, straight-sided bowls, cover with plastic wrap and chill. When thoroughly set, pipe cream over the top of souffles, sprinkle with chopped ginger and decorate with mint sprigs.

Serves 4
Note: Canned mangoes can also be used in this recipe.

MANGO CHARLOTTE

1 packet sponge fingers
⅔ cup caster sugar
3 egg yolks
½ cup milk
½ cup cream
1½ teaspoons vanilla
    essence
3 teaspoons gelatine
1 tablespoon cold water
1 mango, peeled, seeded
    and pureed
1½ cups whipped cream

Garnish
1 small mango, peeled,
    seeded and sliced
½ cup cream, whipped

Line a 22 cm spring-form tin with greaseproof paper. Line the side of the tin with sponge fingers, sugar-coated side outwards. Trim extra biscuits diagonally and wedge between biscuits to hold shape firm, if necessary. Trim fingers 1 cm higher than tin, so that the charlotte will balance when unmoulded.

Beat ½ cup caster sugar and egg yolks in a large mixing bowl until thick and pale. Bring milk, ½ cup cream and 1 teaspoon vanilla essence to boil, remove from heat, cover and set aside to cool.

Slowly stir milk mixture into sugar and eggs. Pour mixture into the top of a double-boiler stirring continuously over simmering water until custard thickens to coat the back of a metal spoon. Remove from heat, leave to cool. Soften gelatine in cold water, then add to custard mixture.

Strain custard into a bowl through a fine sieve and cool in refrigerator to hasten process. Bowl can be placed in a basin containing ice and water. Stir frequently. When mixture starts to set around the edge, fold in mango puree and whipped cream sweetened with 2 tablespoons caster sugar and ½ teaspoon vanilla essence. Pour into tin, filling to the top. Chill in refrigerator a minimum of 2 hours.

Unmould charlotte on a serving plate and decorate with mango slices and extra whipped cream.

Serves 8

HOT ICE CREAM BALLS AND MANGO SAUCE

15 cm diameter sponge
  cake, trimmed into a 13
  × 13 cm square
6 scoops vanilla ice cream
mango slices, to garnish
½ cup flour
¼ cup sifted icing sugar

White Wine Batter
1 cup flour
pinch salt
2½ tablespoons sugar
2 egg yolks
⅔ cups white wine
4 egg whites, whipped

Mango Sauce
1 mango, peeled, seeded
  and sliced
4 tablespoons sugar
2 teaspoons Kirsch
grated chocolate or
  chocolate curls, to
  decorate

Cut sponge into 6 slices and place around the 6 ice cream scoops. Cup the coated balls in hand and press cake firmly in an even circular shape. Place in the freezer until firm.

Roll sponge-coated ice cream balls in flour. Dip in batter, then deep-fry in very hot oil for a couple of seconds each side or until golden brown. Sprinkle fried ice cream balls with icing sugar. Place on dessert plate, pour over the Mango Sauce, decorate with chocolate curls and serve immediately.

White Wine Batter: Mix flour, salt and sugar; add egg yolks and white wine and beat until well combined. Cover and let stand in refrigerator for 1 hour. Before using, fold in whipped egg whites.

Mango Sauce: Blend mango slices, sugar and Kirsch until sugar has dissolved.

Serves 6

MANGO PECAN ICE CREAM

1 litre vanilla ice cream
2 mangoes, peeled, seeded
  and pureed
1 teaspoon lemon juice
1 cup pecan nuts, finely
  chopped

Soften the ice cream slightly, then combine it with the mango puree, lemon juice and nuts. Pour into a freezer tray and freeze until firm.

Serves 4–6

MANGO, PASSIONFRUIT AND HAZELNUT ICE CREAM

1 mango, peeled, seeded
  and roughly chopped
2 passionfruit
½ cup hazelnuts
125 g cream cheese,
  softened
⅓ cup cream
1 cup yoghurt
1 tablespoon honey

Garnish
1 mango, peeled, seeded
  and sliced
mint sprigs

Blend all ingredients, except the sliced mango and mint, until creamy smooth. Pour mixture into freezer trays and freeze until just firm. Remove from freezer and blend again to break up ice crystals.

Allow ice cream to soften a little prior to serving. Serve with mango slices and sprigs of mint.

Serves 4–6

CREAM CHEESE AND MANGO

250 g fresh ricotta cheese
1 teaspoon vanilla essence
4 tablespoons marsala
½ cup cream
2 egg whites
¼ cup caster sugar
grated chocolate or
  chocolate curls, to
  garnish
1 mango, peeled, seeded
  and cut into 6 slices

Mix ricotta, vanilla essence, marsala and cream. Blend for 30 seconds or until ingredients are combined and smooth.

Whisk egg whites until stiff, then gradually add sugar. Fold through ricotta mixture. Spoon into dessert plates and sprinkle with grated chocolate. Arrange a mango slice alongside.

Serves 6

MANGO ICE CREAM

1 mango, peeled, seeded
  and roughly chopped
1 pawpaw, peeled, seeded
  and roughly chopped
1 tablespoon lemon juice
4 egg yolks
⅔ cup icing sugar
¾ cup thickened cream,
  whipped

Puree mango and pawpaw together with lemon juice. Set aside. Combine eggs and icing sugar in the top of a double boiler. Whisk mixture until eggs are pale in colour and thick. Remove from heat and whisk a further 2 minutes.

Fold the fruit puree gently into the egg mixture. Add cream and mix until well blended. Pour into decorative 1 litre metal mould and freeze for a minimum of 3 hours.

To remove, dip the mould in very hot water for 30 seconds before turning out, or scoop out as ice cream balls.

Serves 6–8

Note: Canned mangoes can also be used in this recipe.

TROPICAL ISLAND SORBET

Mango Sorbet
2 mangoes, peeled, seeded
  and pureed
1¼ cups water
⅔ cup caster sugar

Kiwi Fruit Sorbet
4 kiwi fruit, peeled and
  pureed
1¾ cups water
1 cup caster sugar
juice and grated rind 1
  lemon

Pineapple Sorbet
1¾ cups pineapple juice
2–3 drops orange essence
⅔ cup water
⅔ cup caster sugar
fresh mint, to garnish

Spoon the 2 fruit purees and the pineapple juice into 3 separate bowls and set aside.

Sugar syrups: Place water and the required amounts of sugar into 3 separate saucepans. Stir sugar until it dissolves, then boil syrups for mango and kiwi fruit sorbets for 5 minutes. Boil syrup for pineapple sorbet for 3 minutes. Cool syrups, add to their respective purees, and blend.

Add lemon juice and rind to Kiwi Fruit Sorbet and orange essence to Pineapple Sorbet.

Pour mixture into separate freezer trays and freeze for 2½ hours. Remove from freezer and blend to break up the ice crystals. Return to freezer until frozen.

To serve, allow sorbets to soften for 10 minutes at room temperature. Place scoops of sorbet onto chilled trays and return to the freezer for 30 minutes to harden. Arrange the sorbet scoops colourfully on individual serving plates and garnish with fresh mint.

Serves 4–6

Left: Tropical Island Sorbets;
right: Mango Ice Cream

MANGO SORBET

¼ cup sugar
2 mangoes peeled, seeded
   and pureed
¼ cup orange juice
⅓ cup water
2 teaspoons lemon juice
2 egg whites

In a saucepan, combine sugar and mango puree. Bring to boil, stirring constantly. Cover and simmer for 5 minutes. Remove mixture from heat. Add orange juice, water, lemon juice and mix well. Cool slightly.

Pour mixture into a 30 × 20 cm plastic container. Place in freezer until mixture is thick but not set. Whisk egg whites until stiff peaks form. Beat mango mixture until light and frothy, then fold into egg whites. Freeze until firm.

Serves 6
Note: Canned mangoes can also be used in this recipe.

MANGO LIME JELLY WITH PASSIONFRUIT SAUCE

2 passionfruit
½ × 25 g packet lime jelly
   crystals
⅔ cup hot water
⅔ cup cold water
3 mangoes peeled, seeded
   and pureed
juice 1 lime
1 tablespoon gelatine
3 tablespoons hot water

Wet a fluted, 1 litre mould and spoon passionfruit pulp into the bottom.

Dissolve lime jelly crystals in hot water then stir in cold water. Pour into the mould taking care not to disturb passionfruit too much (it helps if you pour the mixture onto the back of a spoon as you add it). Place in refrigerator until set.

Combine mango and lime juice. Dissolve gelatine in hot water and stir into mixture. When lime jelly has set, pour on the mango mixture. Leave in refrigerator for 3 hours or overnight until set.

Serves 4

MANGO PARFAIT

1 tablespoon cornflour
1 cup milk
⅓ cup sugar
1 teaspoon vanilla sugar
250 g ricotta cheese
1½ tablespoons Kirsch
2 mangoes, peeled, seeded,
   diced
50 g chocolate, grated
8 mint leaves, to garnish

Blend cornflour into a paste with 2 tablespoons milk. Combine in a saucepan with remaining milk, sugar and vanilla sugar. Stir until thickened then remove from heat. Cover with plastic wrap to prevent skin forming and cool.

Beat ricotta into the cold custard a little at a time, then add the Kirsch. In long glasses, form layers of Kirsch cream with mango cubes and sprinkle with grated chocolate. Decorate with mint leaves and serve chilled.

AFTER DINNER MANGOES

2 mangoes, peeled, seeded
   and sliced
1 cup water
juice 1 lemon
2 tablespoons Cointreau
200 g caster sugar
1 teaspoon cinnamon

Place mango slices, water, lemon juice and Cointreau in a bowl and leave for 10 minutes.

Drain mangoes, pat dry and place in refrigerator for 5 minutes. Combine sugar and cinnamon in a bowl and toss mango slices until they are well coated. Place slices on a freezing tray, cover and freeze for 3 hours. Serve slices with coffee.

Serves 6

MANGO DELIGHT

1 mango, peeled
¼ cup caster sugar
1 tablespoon Grand
   Marnier
1 egg white, lightly beaten
1 bottle champagne, chilled

Puree mango flesh and combine with sugar and Grand Marnier. Place in large jug or punch bowl.

Frost champagne glasses by dipping in very lightly beaten egg white and then into caster sugar. Chill glasses until required.

Pour chilled champagne onto mango mixture and stir briefly. Pour into frosted glasses and serve.

Serves 6

FRUIT COMPOTE

*2 mangoes, peeled, seeded
   and sliced*
*250 g punnet strawberries,
   hulled*
*1 kiwi fruit, peeled and
   finely sliced*
3 tablespoons sugar
*20 g butter, cut into 1 cm
   cubes*
¼ cup brown sugar
*½ cup orange and mango
   juice*
grated rind 1 orange
¼ teaspoon cinnamon
¼ teaspoon nutmeg
½ cup Madeira
Cointreau, to taste

Sprinkle mangoes, strawberries, and kiwi fruit with sugar and stand for 2 hours then place into a flat baking dish. Dot with butter and bake in an oven preheated to 180°C (350°F) for 5–10 minutes.

Combine brown sugar, orange and mango juice, rind, spices and Madeira in a saucepan. Bring to the boil and keep warm. Scoop fruit into dessert bowls, pour over the sauce, sprinkle over Cointreau to taste.

Serves 4

TROPICAL FRUIT SALAD WITH MANGO CREAM

Fruit Salad
*2 mangoes, peeled, seeded
   and sliced*
*½ small pineapple, peeled
   and cubed*
*2 kiwi fruit, peeled and
   sliced*
*250 g punnet strawberries,
   hulled*
½ cup walnuts
2 passionfruit, to garnish
⅓ cup Cointreau

Mango Cream
*1 mango, peeled, seeded
   and pureed*
*¾ cup thickened cream,
   whipped*

For the salad, put fruit and nuts into a large bowl or 6 individual serving dishes. Pour over Cointreau and refrigerate for 1–2 hours. Serve with Mango Cream topped with passionfruit.
Mango Cream: Fold mango puree through firmly whipped cream.

Serves 6

MANGO SAUTERNE

Prepare the syrup well in advance and chill. Serve preferably in a glass bowl.

1½ cups sauterne
½ cup light brown sugar
2 pieces lemon rind
5 cm piece cinnamon stick
½ large ripe pawpaw
*2 ripe, firm mangoes,
   peeled, seeded and sliced*
*2 punnets strawberries,
   hulled*
*fresh mint leaves, to
   garnish*

To prepare syrup: put sauterne, sugar, lemon rind and cinnamon into a saucepan. Bring to the boil and reduce by half. Strain and refrigerate until cold.

To prepare fruit, peel the pawpaw and cut into large diagonal pieces. Arrange them on the bottom of a serving bowl. Arrange mango slices on top of the pawpaw.

Slice the strawberries lengthwise and scatter them over the mango slices. Pour on the sauterne syrup and chill. Decorate with fresh mint leaves.

Serves 6

FRUITS AU GRATIN

30 g butter
*1 mango, peeled, seeded
   and sliced*
*160 g cherries, stems and
   pits removed*
*1 orange, peeled and
   segmented*
*1 kiwi fruit, peeled and
   sliced*
*1 nectarine, sliced and
   stoned*

Sabayon
2 egg yolks
¼ cup caster sugar
½ teaspoon cornflour
⅓ cup Madeira
brown sugar

Melt butter in pan and saute fruits until heated through. Arrange attractively in 4 individual or 1 large gratin dish and keep warm.

Pour Sabayon over fruits and sprinkle a layer of brown sugar evenly over the top. Heat carefully under preheated grill until sugar melts but does not burn.
Sabayon: Whisk egg yolks and sugar until thick and pale. Blend the cornflour to a paste with a little of the Madeira then whisk into the egg mixture along with the rest of the liquid. Place bowl over a saucepan of simmering water and whisk sauce until frothy.

Serves 4

Sugar and Spice

With its unrivalled attraction simply served as fresh fruit, the mango is not something you might automatically consider putting into a cake, pastry or pudding.

Yet its firm flesh bears up beautifully to baking and its individual taste and aroma can transform a fairly traditional fruitcake or loaf with its exotic tang. Its pliability makes mango a versatile and dependable ingredient and its flavour makes it a must when you are aiming to create a torte with a really distinctive flavour.

Mango Pecan Torte

MACADAMIA AND MANGO CAKE

125 g butter, softened
¾ cup brown sugar
2 eggs
2 cups flour
1 teaspoon allspice
1 teaspoon bicarbonate of
    soda
salt, to taste
½ cup coconut milk
½ cup roasted macadamia
    nuts, chopped
425 g can mango slices,
    drained and pureed
½ mango, peeled, seeded
    and thinly sliced, to
    garnish
whole macadamias, halved
    to garnish

Cream butter and sugar until creamy smooth. Add eggs and beat until well combined. Sift flour, allspice, bicarbonate of soda and salt and fold into creamed mixture alternating with coconut milk. Stir in nuts and mango puree.

Spoon mixture into a greased 22 cm cake tin and arrange mango slices and macadamias decoratively on top. Bake in an oven preheated to 180°C (350°F) for approximately 30 minutes or until a skewer comes out clean when inserted into cake. Store in an airtight container. Serve with butter.

Note: For a higher sided cake, bake for 1 hour in a 20 cm cake tin. This cake is better left 24 hours before serving.

MANGO AND BANANA CAKE

¾ cup peanut oil
3 teaspoons maple syrup
4 tablespoons malt
4 eggs
1½ cups wholemeal flour,
    sifted
4 teaspoons baking powder
1 teaspoon cinnamon, sifted
2 small mangoes, peeled,
    seeded and diced
2 bananas, peeled and diced

To Serve
2 mangoes, peeled, seeded
    and pureed
whipped cream

Beat together oil, maple syrup and malt until light in colour and well mixed with no oil on the surface.

Beat in eggs, one by one. Add flour, baking powder, cinnamon, diced mango and bananas. Pour into a greased and lightly floured 19 cm square cake tin. Bake in an oven preheated to 180°C (350°F) for 30 minutes or until skewer comes out clean when inserted into cake. Serve with mango puree and freshly whipped cream.

FAVOURITE FRUIT CAKE

60 g dried mango pieces
250 g dates, seeded and
    chopped finely
185 g raisins, chopped
60 g glace cherries,
    chopped
125 g slivered almonds
250 g sultanas
250 g currants
1 tablespoon honey
1 tablespoon golden syrup
250 mL orange mango fruit
    juice
1 tablespoon brandy
1 tablespoon rum
250 g butter, softened
1½ cups firmly packed
    brown sugar
4 eggs
1½ cups flour
½ teaspoon allspice
½ teaspoon cinnamon

Combine the mango, dates, raisins, cherries, almonds, sultanas and currants in a bowl. Place honey, syrup, orange mango juice, brandy and rum in a saucepan and heat gently until combined and warm. Pour over fruit and leave overnight.

Cream butter and sugar, add eggs one at a time, stir in fruit then flour and spices. Spoon mixture into a 20 cm tin lined with 2 layers of brown paper. Bake in an oven preheated to 150°C (310°F) for 3–3½ hours or until a skewer comes out clean.

Remove cake from oven, cover with aluminium foil or a tea towel, and leave until cold. Remove from tin and wrap in foil and plastic wrap until required.

MANGO UPSIDE-DOWN CAKE

185 g butter
½ cup sugar
1 cup hazelnuts, toasted
1 mango, peeled, seeded
    and sliced thinly
¾ cup caster sugar
2 eggs, beaten
1 teaspoon instant coffee
½ cup milk
2 cups self-raising flour,
    sifted

Cream 60 g butter and all the sugar; spread over base and sides of a 20 cm tin. Arrange hazelnuts and mangoes decoratively on top.

Cream remaining butter and caster sugar in a bowl, gradually add eggs and beat well. Dissolve coffee in milk, then fold into the mixture alternating with flour.

Pour batter into tin, bake in an oven preheated to 170°C (325°F) for 1¼–1½ hours, until golden. Invert cake onto serving plate and leave for 3 minutes to allow brown sugar mixture to set. Remove cake from oven, cover with aluminium foil and/or a towel and leave until cold. Remove from tin and wrap in foil and plastic wrap until required.

Note: If the cake is to be kept for a long period, pierce holes in the bottom and pour over ½ cup brandy every few weeks. This will keep it moist.

Favourite Fruit Cake

76

1 Line tray with dough, forming a lip

2 Place cherries in a diagonal row

3 Arrange other fruits decoratively

TROPICAL FRUIT CAKE

3 cups water
1½ cups sugar
4 small mangoes, peeled,
   seeded and diced
600 g pineapple, peeled,
   cored and diced
600 g cherries, stalks and
   pips removed
4 cups flour
25 g fresh yeast or 1½ ×
   7 g sachet dry yeast
1 cup milk
3½ tablespoons sugar
1 teaspoon vanilla essence
salt, to taste
125 g butter, cut into small
   pieces
3 tablespoons ground
   hazelnuts

Topping
2 cups flour
1¼ cups brown sugar
1½ teaspoons cinnamon
150 g butter, melted

In a saucepan, combine water and sugar and stir until dissolved. Bring to boil, without stirring for 10 minutes. Remove pan from the heat then steep the mangoes, pineapple and cherries for five minutes each.

Sift flour into bowl and make a well in the centre. Dissolve the yeast in lukewarm milk with 1 teaspoon sugar. Pour into the well and mix together to form a dough. At this stage the dough will look very dry. Lightly oil a clean bowl, put in dough and leave to rise in a warm place until doubled in size.

When the dough has risen sufficiently, add sugar, vanilla, salt, butter and hazelnuts. Work together until dough is smooth and elastic. Place in a lightly greased bowl and leave to rise in a warm place for about 30 minutes.

Knead the dough for 5 minutes and roll out so it is big enough to fit a greased lamington tray. Turn the sides up to form a lip. Cover the dough with the fruits in 3 sections.
Topping: Combine the flour, sugar, cinnamon and butter in a bowl. Rub together with fingers to form crumbs. Sprinkle the crumble mixture evenly over fruit and bake in an oven preheated to 200°C (400°F) for 35–40 minutes.

Makes 24 pieces

Above: Macadamia and Mango Cake;
below: Tropical Fruit Cake

MANGO-FILLED ROLL

¾ cup flour
2 teaspoons baking powder
3 eggs, separated
2 tablespoons hot milk
⅔ cup caster sugar
1 teaspoon cinnamon

Filling

1 cup mango, mashed
1 tablespoon sifted icing
   sugar
2 teaspoons Grand Marnier
1 cup thickened cream,
   well whipped

Grease and line a Swiss roll tin with greased greaseproof paper. Sift flour and baking powder into a bowl. Into another bowl, beat egg yolks one at a time. Fold in flour, baking powder and hot milk.

In a separate bowl, whisk egg whites until thick, then add ⅔ cup sugar gradually until stiff peaks form. Gently fold into cake mixture. Pour mixture into tin and smooth the surface. Bake in an oven preheated to 220°C (425°F) for 8–10 minutes or until golden.

Turn cake out on a sheet of greaseproof paper. Combine 2 tablespoons caster sugar and cinnamon and sprinkle over top. Roll cake up and allow to cool.

Filling: Fold mango, icing sugar and Grand Marnier into cream and chill. Unroll cake and spread with cream. Roll up and chill before serving.

MANGO AND DATE SLICES

1½ cups self-raising
   wholemeal flour
1 cup brown sugar
425 g can mango, drained
   and roughly chopped
½ cup dates, finely
   chopped
½ cup coconut
½ cup hazelnuts, finely
   chopped
185 g butter, melted

Sift flour into bowl, add sugar, mango, dates, coconut and hazelnuts. Mix in butter and pour into a greased lamington tin.

Bake in an oven preheated to 190°C (375F) for 25 minutes. Allow to cool in tin, then cut in pieces and store in an airtight container.

Mango Coconut Log (left); Mango and Date Slices (right); Mango-filled Roll (below)

MANGO PECAN TORTE

2 cups pecan nuts, ground
⅓ cup flour
1 teaspoon unsweetened
   cocoa
salt, to taste
¾ cup sugar
60 g dark chocolate, melted
5 large eggs, separated and
   at room temperature
1 teaspoon vanilla essence
pinch cream of tartar
1 large mango, peeled and
   sliced, to decorate
pecan nuts, to decorate

Buttercream

1 large egg yolk
⅓ cup sugar
1 tablespoon water
15 g chocolate, melted
185 g unsalted butter,
   softened

Combine pecan nuts, flour, cocoa, salt and 2 tablespoons of the sugar and mix well. Add chocolate, egg yolks and vanilla essence and beat until well mixed and smooth. In a clean bowl, whisk egg whites with cream of tartar until stiff, then gradually fold in the remaining sugar. Gently fold both mixtures together.

Butter and flour 2 × 20 cm cake tins and divide the mixture between them. Bake in an oven preheated to 190°C (375°F) for approximately 30 minutes. When cooked, allow cakes to cool then chill in refrigerator.

Spread some of the buttercream over one of the cakes, top with half the mango and place the other cake on top. Spread remaining buttercream over the top and sides of the torte and decorate with whole pecan nuts and remaining mango slices.

Buttercream: Beat egg yolks until thick and pale. Dissolve sugar in water and boil until thick. Pour into beaten egg in a very thin stream, then add chocolate and butter, mixing to form a smooth paste. Chill until firm enough to spread.

Makes 10–12 slices

MANGO COCONUT LOG

¾ cup dried mango slices
½ cup water
¼ cup desiccated coconut
½ cup finely chopped
   almonds
½ cup chopped sultanas
1 tablespoon wheatgerm
1 cup powdered skim milk
½ cup honey
2 teaspoons lemon juice
extra coconut

Chop mango slices into small chunks. Mix well with all ingredients except the extra coconut, then divide mixture into 3 portions. Shape each portion into a 2.5 cm roll, wrap in plastic wrap and chill overnight. To serve, remove wrap, cut in slices and roll in extra coconut.

MANGO LAYER CAKE

Cake Base
1⅔ cups icing sugar
150 g butter, softened
salt, to taste
1 teaspoon vanilla essence
3 eggs
2½ cups flour, sifted
1 teaspoon baking powder,
  sifted

Garnish
mango slices
whipped cream

Filling
1 cup dry white wine
juice and grated rind 1
  lemon
½ cup sugar
3 mangoes, peeled, seeded
  and thinly sliced
1 tablespoon gelatine
2 tablespoons cold water
5 egg yolks
425 g can mango slices,
  drained, juice reserved
  and pureed
2 tablespoons cherry
  liqueur

Beat most of the icing sugar with the butter, salt and vanilla essence until fluffy. Beat in eggs one by one. Add flour and baking powder and mix well.

Butter a 26 cm spring-form tin. Spread ¾ cup mixture over tin and bake in an oven preheated to 190°C (375°F) for 10 minutes. Remove from tin and set aside to cool. Repeat with remaining mixture, buttering the base of the tin each time, to make 5 layers.

Put wine, lemon juice and rind and sugar into a pan and bring to boil. Remove rind and add mango slices. Cook 5 minutes, then leave mango to cool in the syrup.

Beat together egg yolks, 2 tablespoons icing sugar and 2 tablespoons of wine syrup until creamy. Combine egg mixture with remaining wine syrup and cook on low heat, stirring until custard thickens. Allow to cool slightly.

Soften gelatine in cold water then dissolve over pan of simmering water. Stir into egg and wine mixture with mango puree and cherry liqueur. Cover and chill well.

To assemble the cake, place one layer on a plate and cover with ⅕ of the mango slices. Spread ⅕ of the mango cream on top and repeat with remaining layers ending with a layer of cake. Refrigerate for an hour before decorating with mango slices and cream.

Serves 16

MANGO BREAD

2 cups flour
1½ cups sugar
2 teaspoons bicarbonate of
  soda
2 teaspoons cinnamon
½ teaspoon salt
3 eggs

1½ cups diced mango
1 cup salad oil
½ cup grated fresh coconut
½ cup raisins
½ cup chopped macadamia
  nuts
1 teaspoon vanilla essence

Into a bowl sift flour, sugar, bicarbonate of soda, cinnamon and salt. Add remaining ingredients and mix well. Pour into two 19 × 12 cm greased loaf tins. Bake in an oven preheated to 180°C (350°F) for 55 minutes or until bread shrinks away slightly from sides of tin.

Makes 2

MANGO SLICES

¾ cup chopped, dried
  mango
½ cup water
½ cup desiccated coconut
½ cup finely chopped
  almonds

½ cup chopped sultanas
1 tablespoon wheatgerm
1 cup skim milk powder
½ cup honey
2 teaspoons lemon juice
extra coconut, to garnish

Combine all ingredients, then divide mixture into 3 portions. Place on a sheet of foil lightly sprinkled with coconut, fold foil over and shape each portion into a 2.5 cm wide roll. Twist foil ends to seal and chill overnight. To serve, remove foil, dust with extra coconut and cut in slices.

Serves 3

MANGO AND CINNAMON LOAF

125 g softened butter
⅘ cup sugar
1 egg
½ cup natural yoghurt or
  buttermilk
1 cup wholemeal self-
  raising flour

1 cup self-raising flour
½ cup sultanas
½ teaspoon cinnamon
2 small mangoes, peeled,
  seeded and pureed

Combine butter and sugar until creamy. Beat in the egg, then the yoghurt. Blend flours together and sift into mixture. Add sultanas, cinnamon and mango puree.

Pour into a greased loaf tin and cook in an oven preheated to 180°C (350°F) for 1–1½ hours or until golden brown.

Note: A 'saddle of venison' tin can also be used. Grease the tin well and dust with coconut. Leave in the tin a few moments before turning out.

MANGO GINGERBREAD

2 cups peeled and sliced
  fresh mango
1 packet gingerbread mix
2 tablespoons icing sugar
  mixture

Grease and paper line a 20 cm round cake tin. Fill the base with half the mango.

Make the gingerbread mix according to packet instructions and pour into the tin. Bake gingerbread at 180°C (350°F) for 10 minutes.

Remove from oven and arrange rest of mango decoratively on top. Return cake to the oven and bake a further 25 minutes or until a skewer inserted into centre comes out clean. Leave in the tin for 10 minutes before turning out. Sprinkle with icing sugar and serve warm with whipped cream.

Above: Mango and Cinnamon Loaf;
below: Mango Gingerbread

The Pantry Shelf

If you want to score some brownie points then start planning your jam, pickle and chutney-making session for when the mango season is at its peak! Buy in bulk when the fruit is cheap and you'll knock a small fortune off the price of shop-bought versions and have the pleasure of your own cooking into the bargain. These preserves make enormous use of fruit that cannot be used in other recipes, either because they are over or under-ripe, or perhaps because they are bruised or disfigured. They will keep far into the future and enable you to enjoy the fruit of your labours with almost any meal.

Mango Jam

MANGO DATE CHUTNEY

2⅔ cups brown sugar
2½ cups white wine
  vinegar
3 large green mangoes,
  peeled, seeded and finely
  chopped
1 teaspoon finely chopped
  ginger root
6 cloves garlic, crushed
1 cinnamon stick
125 g dates, seeded and
  chopped

Combine sugar and vinegar in a heavy-based saucepan and stir until sugar has dissolved. Bring to boil and add mangoes. Add remaining ingredients and boil again. Reduce heat and simmer 1½ hours until chutney is very thick. Take out cinnamon stick and spoon into sterilised jars.

Remove any air bubbles by piercing mixture with a skewer. Cut out circles of greaseproof paper according to jar size. Place these on top of chutney and press lightly with fingertips to remove air. Seal with sterilised lids. Store in a cool place and refrigerate after opening.
  Makes 12 litres
Note: This recipe can easily be halved.

HOT MANGO CHUTNEY

5 red chillies, sliced and
  seeded
5 green chillies, sliced and
  seeded
½ cup chopped garlic
½ cup chopped ginger root
½ cup fresh coriander
2 tablespoons oil
¼ cup ground cumin

1 tablespoon white cumin
  seeds
½ cup desiccated coconut
2 tablespoons black
  mustard seeds
12 green mangoes, peeled,
  seeded and diced
2½ cups malt vinegar
salt, to taste (optional)

Blend chillies, garlic, ginger and coriander to a smooth puree. Heat oil in a large heavy-based saucepan and fry pureed ingredients with the ground cumin, cumin seeds, coconut and mustard seeds. Fry 2 minutes. Add mangoes and vinegar, bring to boil then reduce heat and simmer, uncovered, until mixture is thick and pulpy, approximately 40–50 minutes. Add salt if desired.

Bottle chutney in sterilised jars. Remove any air bubbles by piercing mixture with a skewer. Cut out circles of greaseproof paper according to jar size. Place these on top of the hot chutney and press lightly with fingertips to remove air. Seal with sterilised lids and store in a cool place. Refrigerate after opening.
Makes 2 litres
Note: This recipe can easily be halved.

CHILLIES FOR CHUTNEY

Great care must be taken when cutting chillies. Either wear protective gloves or wash hands thoroughly after cutting.

SPICY MANGO AND APPLE CHUTNEY

1 medium-sized firm under-
  ripe mango
4 apples, peeled, cored and
  diced
2 cloves garlic, minced
2 onions, chopped
2 capsicums, seeded and
  chopped

4 red chillies, seeded and
  sliced
2 tablespoons chopped
  coriander
¼ teaspoon cayenne
  pepper
2 cups malt vinegar
1 cup brown sugar
salt, to taste

Place all ingredients in a heavy-based saucepan. Mix well and bring to boil, then simmer gently for 10 minutes. Reduce heat to low and cook, stirring until mangoes are soft, the apples are tender and mixture is jam-like in consistency. Add salt to taste.

Remove from heat and cool slightly. Bottle chutney in sterilised jars. Remove any air bubbles by piercing mixture with a skewer. Cut out circles of greaseproof paper according to jar size. Place these on top of the chutney and press lightly with fingertips to remove air. Seal with sterilised lids. Store in a cool place and refrigerate after opening.
  Makes 1.7 litres

MANGO AND TOMATO CHUTNEY

6 mangoes, peeled, seeded
  and diced
6 under-ripe tomatoes,
  sliced
6 onions, sliced
2 cup raisins
2 cups currants
4 cups brown sugar
3 cups malt vinegar
1 red or green chilli, seeded
  and sliced
salt, to taste

Put all ingredients into a heavy-based saucepan and bring to boil. Reduce heat and simmer gently for 30 minutes. Add salt if desired.

Remove from heat. Bottle chutney in sterilised jar. Remove any air bubbles by piercing mixture with a skewer. Cut out circles of greaseproof paper according to jar size. Place these on top of chutney and press lightly with fingertips to remove air. Seal with sterilised lids. Store in a cool place. Refrigerate after opening.
  Makes 1.7 litres

MANGO NECTARINE CHUTNEY

5 mangoes, peeled, seeded
   and roughly chopped
4 nectarines, halved,
   seeded
¼ teaspoon finely chopped
   ginger root
1 onion, chopped
1 cup brown sugar
½ cup white wine vinegar
2 teaspoons chilli powder
salt, to taste

Blend mangoes, nectarines, ginger and onion for 30 seconds, until ingredients are finely chopped. Place in a heavy-based pan with sugar, vinegar and chilli powder. Mix well, bring to boil and simmer gently for 10 minutes. Reduce heat to low and continue to stir and cook until mangoes and nectarines are soft and the mixture is jam-like in consistency. Add salt to taste.

Remove pan from heat and cool slightly. Ladle chutney into sterilised jars. Remove any air bubbles by piercing mixture with a skewer. Cut out circles of greaseproof paper according to jar size. Place these on the top of chutney and press lightly with finger tips to remove air. Seal with sterilised lids. Refrigerate after opening.

Makes 1 litre

MANGO NUT CHUTNEY

6 medium-sized green
   mangoes, peeled and
   sliced
salt, to taste
4 cloves garlic
1 tablespoon chopped
   ginger root
6 large dry red chillies
2½ cups malt vinegar
1½ cups sugar
60 almonds, blanched and
   chopped
125 g raisins

Sprinkle sliced mangoes with salt. Grind the garlic, ginger and chillies to a paste with a little vinegar. Boil remaining vinegar, add sugar and mangoes, and cook for 5 minutes over low heat. Add garlic, ginger and chilli paste and cook for 10 minutes. Stir in almonds and raisins and cook another 5 minutes. Add salt to taste, cool and bottle in sterilised jars.

Remove any air bubbles by piercing mixture with a skewer. Cut out circles of greaseproof paper according to jar size. Place these on top of chutney and press lightly with fingertips to remove air. Seal with sterilised lids. Store in a cool place and refrigerate after opening.

Makes 1.5 litres

MANGO WALNUT CHUTNEY

1.75 litres malt vinegar
1.75 kg sugar
3 large green mangoes,
   peeled, seeded and
   roughly chopped
2 large Spanish onions
2 cloves garlic, crushed
1-2 red chillies, sliced and
   seeded
2 tablespoons chopped
   ginger root
1 teaspoon cinnamon
1 teaspoon nutmeg
1⅔ cups sultanas
1½ cups walnuts, ground
salt, to taste

Combine vinegar and sugars in a heavy-based saucepan over moderate heat. Stir to dissolve sugar, bring to boil and boil 20 minutes without stirring. Add remaining ingredients and simmer for 1½–2 hours, stirring occasionally. Spoon into hot sterilised jars.

Remove any air bubbles by piercing mixture with a skewer. Cut out circles of greaseproof paper according to jar size. Place these on top of chutney and press lightly with fingertips to remove air. Seal with sterilised lids. Store in a cool place and refrigerate after opening.

Makes approximately 2 litres

MANGO COULIS

½ capsicum, seeded and
   diced
1 carrot, diced
1 onion, quartered
½ cup parsley
bouquet garni
1 clove garlic
1½ cups white wine
salt, to taste
2 mangoes, peeled, seeded
   and pureed
1 tablespoon Cointreau

Mix capsicum, carrot, onion, parsley, bouquet garni, wine and salt in a heavy-based saucepan, bring to boil and simmer for 10 minutes. Alternatively, put ingredients into a microwave-safe bowl and cook for 3 minutes on High.

Drain, reserving liquid and discarding vegetables. Put liquid and mango into a saucepan and heat through. Add Cointreau and serve. Store in refrigerator.

Makes 3 cups

MANGO JAM

4–5 mangoes to make 4
  cups pulp, peeled, seeded
  and chopped
2 cups sugar
juice ½ lemon

Place mango in a pan with sugar and lemon. Bring to boil, and cook, stirring from time to time, until jam thickens. Pour into hot sterilised jars, seal and store in a cool place.
  Makes 1½ cups

MANGO AND STRAWBERRY JAM

3 mangoes, peeled, seeded
  and diced
250 g punnet strawberries,
  hulled and quartered
1⅗ cups sugar
juice 1 lemon

In a heavy-based saucepan, combine mangoes, strawberries, sugar and lemon juice. Cook over moderate heat, stirring to dissolve sugar. Bring to boil and simmer 30–35 minutes until the jam is thick.

Pour into hot sterilised jars. Cut out circles of greaseproof paper according to jar size. Place these on the top of hot jam and press lightly with finger tips to remove air. Seal with sterilised lids. Store in a cool place.

  Makes approximately 3 cups

MANGO SEAFOOD MAYONNAISE

2 egg yolks at room
  temperature
½ teaspoon dry mustard
salt, to taste
1 cup olive oil
1–2 tablespoons lemon
  juice
sugar, to taste
1 mango, peeled, seeded
  and pureed
¼–½ teaspoon lemon
  pepper

Combine egg yolks, mustard and salt in bowl. Whisk with a balloon whisk until thick and pale. Add oil drop by drop, whisking constantly until all the oil has been incorporated and mixture is smooth. Whisk in remaining ingredients. Alternatively, this procedure can be followed using a food processor. Store in refrigerator until required. Serve as an accompaniment to prawns and lobster.
  Makes 1½ cups

FRESH BASIL AND MANGO VINAIGRETTE

2 tablespoons safflower oil
1 tablespoon lemon juice
2 slices mango or more
2 teaspoons white wine
  vinegar
1–2 fresh basil leaves
salt and freshly ground
  pepper, to taste

In a blender, combine all ingredients, adding enough mango to thicken vinaigrette. Serve chilled with salad.
  Makes ½ cup
Note: Canned mangoes can also be used. 1 can = 1 mango.

SPICY MANGO SAUCE

2 mangoes, peeled, seeded
  and pureed
1 tablespoon Madeira
50 g butter
2 green chillies, finely
  chopped
1 teaspoon caraway seeds
salt and freshly ground
  pepper, to taste

Combine mango and Madeira until smooth. Melt butter in a pan, add all ingredients, cover and simmer 8 minutes, stirring. If sauce becomes too thick, thin with a little water. Store in refrigerator. Serve hot or cold with beef, pork, fish, chicken and rice dishes.
  Makes approximately 1½ cups

MANGO RHUBARB SAUCE

2 stalks rhubarb, chopped
¼ cup water
2 × 500 g firm but under-
  ripe mangoes, peeled,
  seeded and pureed
1 tablespoon lemon juice
1 teaspoon coriander
½ cup walnuts, ground
¼ cup sugar

Place rhubarb and water in a heavy-based saucepan and simmer, covered, for 10 minutes until rhubarb is tender. Add remaining ingredients and simmer gently over a low heat for 30 minutes. Remove from heat.

Bottle sauce in sterilised jars. Remove any air bubbles by piercing mixture with a skewer. Cut out circles of greaseproof paper according to jar size. Place these on the top of sauce and press lightly with fingertips to remove air. Seal with sterilised lids and refrigerate.
  Makes 2½ cups

Left to right: Spicy Mango Sauce; Mango Garlic Sauce; Mango Seafood Mayonnaise; Honeyed Mango Sauce

MANGO SAUCE

1 cup dry white wine
½ cup cream
1 mango, peeled and sliced

Pour wine and cream into a saucepan. Bring to boil and continue boiling until sauce lightly coats the back of the spoon. Add mango slices, heat through and serve with roast turkey.

Makes 2 cups

HONEYED MANGO SAUCE

2 large mangoes, peeled
* and seeded*
2 teaspoons honey
juice 1 lemon
½ teaspoon grated ginger
* root*

Puree all ingredients together until smooth and refrigerate. Serve with fresh fruit, ice cream, puddings and crepes.

Makes 1½ cups

MANGO GARLIC SAUCE

40 g butter
2 cloves garlic, minced
2 mangoes, peeled, seeded
* and pureed*
1 tablespoon lemon juice
2 shallots, finely sliced
1 tablespoon fresh cream

Melt butter in pan, add garlic and saute until tender. Add mango puree and lemon juice, then simmer gently for 5 minutes. Stir in shallots and cream. Add a little water if sauce is too thick. Store in refrigerator until serving time.

Makes 1½ cups

Something Cool

Mangoes have a great deal of juice, which makes them an ideal ingredient in cool summer drinks. Unlike many fruits, which collapse into watery blandness when pureed, mango retains its colour and bulk, as well as that stunning flavour. For these reasons, it can be served as readily in non-alcoholic drinks as in alcoholic cocktails. Remember, however, that the wonderful fruit flavour can mask the intoxicating effects of a real punch packer!

MANGO MINT COOLER

1 mango, peeled, seeded
   and pureed
2 tablespoons Creme de
   Menthe
3 tablespoons Advocaat
½ cup orange and mango
   juice
½ cup lemonade
mint leaves, to garnish

Combine all ingredients and blend until smooth. Pour into tall glasses over ice. Garnish with mint leaves.
   Serves 2

TROPICAL MANGO PUNCH

2 mangoes, peeled, seeded
   and roughly chopped
2 cups pineapple juice
1 cup vodka
½ cup lemon juice
1 tablespoon caster sugar
20 ice cubes
lemon slices, to garnish

Combine first 5 ingredients and blend until smooth. Serve immediately over ice cubes garnished with lemon slices.
   Serves 8–10
Note: Mixture will settle after a short time and may look like it has separated; simply stir.

MANGO COCONUT ICE

½ cup crushed ice
2 tablespoons gin
dash Fraise de Bois or 1
    strawberry
½ mango, peeled, seeded
    and chopped
2 tablespoons thick coconut
    cream
lemon juice, to taste

Garnish
mint leaves
2 strawberries

Fill the blender with crushed ice and pour in the gin and
liqueur. Add the mango, coconut cream and lemon juice,
and blend for several seconds until smooth. Pour into
champagne glasses and garnish with mint leaves and
whole strawberries.
    Serves 2

MANGO COMBO

425 g can mango slices,
    juice reserved
1 cup natural yoghurt
1 cup crushed ice
½ teaspoon ground
    cardamom seeds, to
    garnish

Combine all ingredients and blend for 30 seconds or until
creamy smooth. Pour into tall glasses and sprinkle cardamom on top.
    Serves 2

MANGO RUM ICE

1 small mango, peeled,
    seeded and sliced
½ cup light rum
1½ tablespoons lime juice
1 tablespoon caster sugar
    or sweetener, to taste
1 cup crushed ice
mint sprigs, to garnish

Combine all ingredients and blend until smooth. Pour into
chilled cocktail glasses and serve.
    Serves 2

MANGO TREAT

1 mango, peeled, seeded
    and mashed
⅓ cup orange and mango
    juice
⅓ cup light cream
¼ cup Advocaat
mint leaves, to garnish

Combine all ingredients and blend until smooth. Pour into
tall glasses over ice. Garnish with mint leaves.
    Serves 2

Left to right: Mango Mint Cooler;
Mango Rum Ice; Caribbean Mango;
Tropical Mango Punch; Mango Treat;
Champagne Mango

TANGY MANGO COOLER

250 g mango, peeled,
    seeded and roughly
    chopped
1 teaspoon grated lemon
    rind
juice 1 lemon
½ cup buttermilk
1 cup crushed ice
sweetener, to taste
mint sprig, to garnish

Combine first 6 ingredients and blend for 30 seconds or
until creamy smooth. Garnish with mint.
    Serves 1

MINTY MANGO WHIP

1 mango, peeled, seeded
    and cut into chunks
2 scoops vanilla ice cream
mint, to garnish

Blend all ingredients until smooth. Pour into tall chilled
glasses and garnish with sprigs of mint.
    Serves 1

CHAMPAGNE MANGO

3 mangoes, peeled, seeded
    and sliced
1 bottle semi-sweet
    champagne

Place mango slices in glasses. Just before serving, pour on
iced champagne.
    Serves 4

MANGO SMOOTHIE

1 mango, peeled, seeded
    and pureed
1 cup yoghurt
¼ cup ice cream
1 teaspoon honey
chopped nuts, to garnish
    (optional)

Combine all ingredients except nuts. Blend until smooth.
Serve with a sprinkling of chopped nuts if desired.
    Serves 2

CARIBBEAN MANGO

2 mangoes
1 cup milk
juice 3 limes or 4 lemons
1 teaspoon grated lime or
    lemon rind
½ cup caster sugar
1 cup crushed ice

Garnish
4 lime or lemon slices
mint sprigs

Combine all ingredients and blend for 20–30 seconds until
smooth and creamy. Pour into chilled glasses and garnish
with lime slices.
    Serves 4

ICE CREAM MANGO WHIP

2 mangoes, peeled, seeded
    and chopped
1 cup milk
1 tablespoon maple syrup
3 drops almond essence
2 cups strawberry ice
    cream

Combine first 4 ingredients and blend until smooth. Add
ice cream and blend for 10 seconds more. Serve immediately.
    Serves 4–6

MANGO AND COCONUT DELIGHT

2 mangoes, peeled, seeded
    and roughly chopped
1 cup coconut milk
juice 1 lemon and grated
    rind ½ lemon
sweetener, to taste
vanilla essence, to taste
1 cup crushed ice

Garnish
6 thin slices lemon
mint sprigs

Combine all ingredients and blend for 20–30 seconds or
until smooth and creamy. Pour into tall chilled glasses.
Garnish with lemon slices and mint sprigs.
    Serves 6

Ice Cream Mango Whip

MANGO MILKSHAKE

2 cups milk
2 mangoes, peeled, seeded
   and sliced
vanilla essence, to taste
2 scoops vanilla ice cream

Combine all ingredients and blend until smooth. Decorate 2 long glasses with coloured sugar crystals, pour in the blended ingredients and serve.
   Serves 2

MANGO SLIMMER

⅓ cup natural low-fat
   yoghurt
½ mango, peeled, seeded
   and pureed
⅔ cup chilled mineral
   water or soda water
nutmeg, to taste
mint sprig, to garnish

Combine yoghurt and mango puree in a tall glass. Stir in mineral water and add a few ice-cubes. Garnish with a sprig of mint.
   Makes 1 cup

MANGO PUNCH REFRESHER

1 mango, peeled, seeded
   and pureed
4 passionfruit, pulp
   removed
3 mint leaves, finely
   chopped
1 litre orange and mango
   juice
1 litre ginger beer
3 cups wild apple tea,
   frozen into ice trays or
   3 cups black tea

Combine all ingredients and blend until ice cubes have broken up.
   Makes 3 litres

MANGO CITRUS CUP

1 sweet navel or Valencia
   orange
2 sugar cubes
2 cups mango juice
1 cup orange juice
½ cup lemon juice
750 mL bottle mineral
   water
fresh mint leaves, to
   garnish

Wash and dry the orange, then pierce all over with a fork or skewer. Rub sugar cubes over the orange until the cubes are orange in colour. Juice orange and combine all ingredients and blend for 30 seconds or until creamy smooth. Chill well. Pour into tall glasses and garnish with a mint leaf.
   Makes 1.5 litres

GRAND MARNIER AND CHAMPAGNE MANGO

1 mango, peeled, seeded
   and roughly chopped
⅓ cup caster sugar
1 tablespoon Grand
   Marnier
750 mL bottle chilled
   champagne
mint sprigs, to garnish

Combine the first 3 ingredients and blend until smooth. Divide mango mixture between glasses and top up with chilled champagne. Garnish with mint sprigs.
   Serves 4–6

For Your Information

GLOSSARY OF TERMS

AUSTRALIA	UK	USA
Equipment and terms		
can	tin	can
crushed	minced	pressed
frying pan	frying pan	skillet
grill	grill	broil
greaseproof paper	greaseproof paper	waxproof paper
lamington tin	oven tray, 4 cm deep	oven tray, 1½ in deep
paper cases	paper baking cases	
paper towel	kitchen paper	white paper towel
patty tin	patty tin	muffin pan
plastic wrap	cling film	plastic wrap
punnet	punnet	basket for 250 g fruit
sandwich tin	sandwich tin	layer cake pan
seeded	stoned	pitted
spring-form cake tin	loose bottomed cake tin	
Swiss roll tin	Swiss roll tin	jelly roll pan
Ingredients		
bacon rasher	bacon rasher	bacon slice
beetroot	beetroot	beets
bicarbonate of soda	bicarbonate of soda	baking soda
black olive	black olive	ripe olive
capsicum	pepper	sweet pepper
caster sugar	caster sugar	granulated table sugar
cornflour	cornflour	cornstarch
cream	single cream	light or coffee cream
crystallised fruit	crystallised fruit	candied fruit
desiccated coconut	desiccated coconut	shredded coconut
eggplant	aubergine	eggplant
essence	essence	extract
five spice	Chinese spice combination of cinnamon, cloves, fennel, star anise and Szechuan pepper	
flour	plain flour	all-purpose flour
glace cherry	glace cherry	candied cherry
green cabbage	white or roundhead cabbage	
hundreds and thousands	hundreds and thousands	non pareils
icing sugar	icing sugar	confectioners' sugar
pawpaw	pawpaw	papaya or papaw
pickled pork	gammon	
prawn	prawn or shrimp	shrimp
rock melon	ogen melon	cantaloupe
self-raising flour	self-raising flour	all-purpose flour with baking powder, 1 cup: 2 teaspoons
shallot	spring onion	scallion
snow pea	mangetout, sugar pea	snow pea
stock cube	stock cube	bouillon cube
sultanas	sultanas	seedless white or golden raisins
tasty cheese	mature Cheddar	
thickened cream	double cream	heavy or whipping cream
tomato puree	tomato puree	tomato paste
tomato sauce	tomato sauce	tomato ketchup
unsalted butter	unsalted butter	sweet butter
wholemeal flour	wholemeal flour	wholewheat flour
yoghurt	natural yoghurt	unflavoured yoghurt
zucchini	courgette	zucchini

OVEN TEMPERATURES

	Celsius	Fahrenheit
Very slow	120	250
Slow	140–150	275–300
Moderately slow	160	325
Moderate	180	350
Moderately hot	190	375
Hot	200	400
	220	425
	230	450
Very hot	250–260	475–500

MEASUREMENTS

Standard Metric Measures

1 cup	=	250 mL
1 tablespoon	=	20 mL
1 teaspoon	=	5 mL

All spoon measurements are level

CUP MEASURES

1 x 250 mL cup =	Grams	Ounces
breadcrumbs, dry	125	4½
soft	60	2
butter	250	8¾
cheese, grated		
cheddar	125	4½
coconut, desiccated	95	3¼
flour, cornflour	130	4¾
plain or self-raising	125	4½
wholemeal	135	4¾
fruit, mixed dried	160	5¾
honey	360	12¾
sugar, caster	225	7¾
crystalline	250	8¾
icing	175	6¾
moist brown	170	6
nuts	125	4

If you need to substitute

Fresh fruit: replace with canned or tinned fruit.

Fresh herbs: replace with a quarter of the recommended quantity of dried herbs.

Mulberries: replace with blackcurrants.

Pecans: replace with walnuts.

Rock melons: replace with honeydew melons.

Snapper: replace with any firm white fish such as haddock, cod or whiting.

Index

ACKNOWLEDGEMENTS

The publisher would like to
thank the following for their
assistance during the
production of this book:
Decor Gifts for glassware
(pages 90, 91)
Hale Imports Pty Ltd for
tableware (page 37)
Johnson's Overalls Pty Ltd for
cutlery (pages 25, 37, 79)
Lifestyle Imports Pty Ltd for
tableware (pages 12, 25, 41,
53, 62, 75, 80, 83)
Made Where for cutlery
(pages 15, 28, 30, 34, 84)
Mikasa Tableware for
tableware (pages 27, 28, 49,
50, 51, 80)
Joan Monks of Q.U.F.
Industries for her Favourite
Fruit Cake (page 76)
Sasaki for tableware (pages 20,
22, 30, 34, 50, 51, 70)
Villa Italiana for tableware
(pages 19, 43, 47, 56, 57, 59,
84)